"In order to dare we must know;
in order to will we must dare;
we must will to possess empire and
to reign we must be silent."

Aleister Crowley

Becoming Witch

Back to the Basics

CricketSong

Printed by Kindle Direct Publishing

Copyright © 2020 by Sheri Breault Kreitner

ISBN- 9798650904816

First edition

Cover design by Enrique M. Torres
Interior illustrations by Nakita Melo

Typeset in Times New Roman

Printed in United States of America

This book is dedicated to all who identify as Witch.
May you transcend in your becoming.

Acknowledgments

My personal journey in becoming Witch has spanned over a number of years and during this profound time I have been fortunate to share personal experiences with a number of individuals, some who openly identify as Witch and others who do not (though I would suggest that they hold some bit of Witchiness within them) who have in some fashion influenced my practice and flavored the Witch I am actively becoming today. Whether these individuals are conscious of their contribution or not, I would like to take a moment to acknowledge their impact on my Craft:

My soul sister, Erin Fallon-Sullivan, my Anam Cara, my beloved, who awakened my Witch-self, enabling me to possess the courage to pursue my Truth, whatever it looked like even if it wasn't a direct reflection of her own. You are Hillary to my CC; Gillian to my Sally; I will love you, always and forever, from one incarnation to the next.

My husband, Alex, my best-friend and soulmate, for his endless love and support as he continues to encourage me to overcome any obstacles I encounter and push through any perceived resistance I experience, allowing me to continue my journey in becoming Witch. For all this I am eternally grateful.

I would also like to thank: Xanna, Donna, Ladye Morgandy, Lady Gwen, The LoonWitch, previous Lunar Wisdom Coven members and Wisdom of the Crescent Moon members, Cristina, Karren, Celine, Anni, Jacqui, Annika, Tara, Renee, and the Witches within the YouTube community and those within the Pagan community in the state of Massachusetts.

Contents

Introduction

I was aware that transitions were challenging, I had been through life transitions before. I attended four years of college away from home in another state, moved to another part of my home state after I graduated, I had been married and divorced twice, before I met and was legally handfasted my current husband, I had been pregnant three times, experienced one miscarriage, during which I was convinced I would die, gave birth twice, and after my second baby, fell into the darkest and seemingly endless hole of Post-Partum Depression. I was familiar with life transitions, and though none of my experiences were easy, I had endured.

I understood that sometimes, for some people, life transitions could be extremely difficult and all sorts of messy, but I realize now, as I consider the last couple of years of my life, I was naïve to think that my most recent transition, a relocation from Massachusetts to Washington state, was going to be easy and smooth. I thought that because I had been preparing and organizing for nearly a year, a simple change in address wouldn't make any great impact on my life or my Witchcraft. I was seriously mistaken.

This book is a result of that transition and the tremendous influence it had on my Craft. I was forced to go "*back to the basics*" of my own practice and to take the time to contemplate and evaluate what remained True for me and what no longer served my Will as Witch, then I was required to make the necessary changes that were demanded in order for my magick to be effective and successful once more. I truly believe that revisiting the basics can be beneficial for all Witches, especially after any impactful transition, even if the transition seems to be typically mundane in its nature. As Witch, everything we encounter influences our Craft, whether we are conscious of it or not.

I believe that it's always imperative for the Witch to ask her or himself: "Why do I do what I do?" "What is the reason for doing this in this way or for using that correspondence in this spell?" And I don't believe that the answer should be as simple as: "I saw PureWytch do it in her YouTube video." or "The author of this popular Witchy book told me to use it." Those aren't beneficial to the Witch's growth within their practice. There is no wisdom or personal understanding contained within those reasons. In the process of getting "*back to the basics*" I will ask you to consider your reasons and evaluate your motives and beliefs as I did with myself.

Please keep in mind that this book was not written for the inexperienced Witch, someone just beginning their research on Witchcraft and considering if this is where they belong. While I do discuss the basics of magick and Witchcraft, this is not a beginner book; there are plenty of those already published and available for online purchase. This book was written for an audience of Witches, such as myself, who at one time had an active, if not thriving practice, and then experienced some type of life transition that resulted in inactivity, stagnation, or doubt, and are currently seeking to reestablish their Craft and once more regain their personal power, the power of the Witch.

This book was written by someone, like you, with the hope that after you've read through these pages and have practiced, to some extent, the suggested exercises, you will rediscover your power and skills with magick and efficiently anchor yourself in the basics of your own Witchcraft, allowing you to continue on your journey in becoming Witch.

Blessed Be!
CricketSong

Exercise: Selecting Your Journal

At the end of each chapter included in this work you will find exercises designed specifically for you that correspond with the topic of the chapter. It is my desire that after you have finished reading the presented information, which includes my personal thoughts, perspectives, and opinion of the topics, you will engage with the exercises. My goal is that, through them, you will explore the concept further and uncover personal thoughts, feelings, and beliefs that perhaps you hadn't considered, or gain a deeper understanding of topics you already had a firm grasp on, or discover a new way in which to practice your Craft.

To begin your journey with getting back to the basics you will need a journal in which to track your progress. Whether you decide to use your existing Book of Shadows, Book of Mirrors, Book of Light, Book of Illuminations, Grimoire, or other type of Witchy journal, an online blog, a simple Word document, or believe it's best to begin with a new journal you just bought at Barnes & Noble, this first exercise for you is to decide where you will record your responses, track your progress, and write about your experiences. It is helpful and of great benefit to the Witch to have this information collected in one place where you are able to look back and read what you had experienced days, weeks, months, or even years later. Consider this journal to be your personal resource holding insight about yourself and your beliefs that you may not be aware of at the time you record the information.

When I first began my journey as Witch, I used a black and white college ruled composition book for my Book of Shadows. It was inexpensive and easily obtainable, but still served the purpose of holding my experiences, thoughts, insights, and research. A few months later, at a local metaphysical shop, I was able to find a black leather-bound journal with an embossed pentacle on the cover. I loved it and purchased it without hesitation, thinking that it would be my forever journal, the one I would eventually pass to my children when I died. I began transcribing all the information from my composition book into my new "forever" journal. I was naïve. As time passed, I continued to study and learn about Witchcraft as well as other occult paths and topics, which lead me to gather more information and material from various sources. I was also participating and leading rituals and casting spells, which required me to keep records of the magickal workings. I quickly discovered that my tendency to reorganize the information was not ideal with my "forever" bound journal. I ended up with pages ripped out from one place and taped into a different spot, making my beautiful journal appear messy. It just wasn't working for me. I needed a book that allowed me add pages wherever I wanted and to move preexisting pages from one place to another without ripping and taping.

The need for clean organization led me to a three-ring binder. They worked for me in high school so I knew they would work for me then, but I wanted my magickal binder to be less mundane and more witchy.

I had experience in crafting keepsake photo albums, three-ring binders decorated for weddings or baby showers, so I used that experience to make my binder more witchy. I cut out a pentacle in a piece of corrugated cardboard and hot-glued it to the plastic cover of the binder. I purchased a yard of imitation leather from the fabric store and used it to cover the entire binder. I purchased satin ribbon, which matched the color of the imitation leather, and glued it over the edges of the fabric and used it to hold the binder closed. I was pleased with the results and found that this type of journal not only served my needs, but other Witches found them to be helpful as well, and I crafted many of them for friends and customers over the years.

My most current journal, which includes all information from my previous journals, is in digital format.

Once you have made the decision as to which type of journal you will use, which I encourage you to make with intention and not with a careless impulse, I want you to dedicate the first entry on the first page of the journal to the journey we will be taking together as you read and work through this book. The dedication should take whatever form you desire; a work of prose, a poem, freethought, or even a drawing, if you are so inclined. There really is no wrong way to do this exercise, unless you are doing it without intention.

Consider this first entry a type of consecration or blessing for your journal. The following is my entry:

April 25, 2020

Hearken this solitary Witch's call,
From grassy fields to Willows tall.
Hail spirits of North, East, South, and West.
It is your guidance I do request.

Spirits of Earth I ask of thee,
Your humble daughter, please share with me,
Your abundant powers of protection,
As I bare my Shadows for introspection.

Spirits of Air I ask of thee,
Your humble daughter, please share with me,
Your powers of knowledge and insight.
Upon the words I think and write.

Spirits of Fire I ask of thee,
Your humble daughter, please share with me,
Your powers of courage, passion, and Will,
So that I am brave when I must remain still.

Spirits of Water I ask of thee,
Your humble daughter, please share with me,
Your powers of reason and intuition,
To evaluate my own condition.

This is my request, this is my plea,
As I Will it, so mote it be.

Chapter 1

Words Hold Power

I begin most, if not all, conversations I engage in, all live streams I host on YouTube, and videos I upload to various online platforms, by establishing a clear definition for the term or topic I will be discussing. I find that by clearly stating the definition I'm establishing a common ground where all involved in the conversation can meet and hopefully begin a fruitful dialogue. Ideally, any confusion that might have happened if we were all using our own definitions or understandings of the term or word that I have brought forward to discuss, will have been curbed and instead the discussion will be beneficial, bringing forth new thoughts, insights, and opinions that enable each participant to experience personal growth and expansion.

When getting *"back to the basics"* of your Craft, I believe that this process of defining some common concepts and popular terms used within the magickal community is an important step that you would benefit from as you spend time considering and perhaps even researching the terms. There is no *"one size fits all*" definition that will be suitable for every Witch and her or his practice. Our Craft is as unique as we are; no two Witches' practices appears the same. There is no one way to practice, no one way to live, no one way to becoming Witch, so it's vital to take the time to consider your thoughts, feelings, and beliefs about these concepts and terms, if only for yourself. Each Witch evolves in their own time and in their own way, this transformation is a reflection of what we think, what we feel, what we believe, and experience.

I realize that there will be individuals reading my words who will resist the idea of defining anything pertaining to themselves or their practice because they hold the belief that labels restrain them in some way and that to adopt a title for themselves or to define their practice with a word, whether simple and common or complex and unusual, will limit their magick. While I can certainly understand this perspective, I disagree. I would suggest that by merely picking up this book in whatever form you are reading it, you have, in some way, even if only to yourself, labeled yourself. You have identified as Witch, because that very word is part of the title of this book: *Becoming Witch*. The word holds a meaning for who you are or who you desire to be. It is a label you associate with in some way. It is you; you are Witch.

We should also consider the fact that you already possess a label, one that others know you by: your name. It might have been given to you at birth by your parents, or bestowed upon you by a High Priestess or the gods themselves, or adopted by you in some ritualistic way. That name is a definition of who you are, and yes, I agree, that the name may restrain you, but you do have the freedom to change it if you desire. The name may also have the ability to grant you additional power that would be unattainable to you if you didn't possess it. Words, names, labels, titles – they all hold a power; a vibration that can affect the one who possesses it.

We are physical beings and we perceive ourselves as independent from each other, this begins to happen during our first year of life when we understand that we are separate from our mother and begin to establish our own unique personality. Our personality is unlike anyone else's, shaped by the experiences we find pleasurable and distasteful, our characteristics and qualities, our past and current life experiences. This process of building a distinct cohesive sense of self continues throughout our physical lifetime. It establishes a boundary and separation in the unity of All There Is. You, me, us, we, he, she, them … they are all labels, which yes, can be limiting, but don't necessarily have to be.

I propose that defining yourself and your practice can be limiting, labeling can be restricting, but as Witches we are aware of this possibility and have the ability to shed a label when it no longer serves us. We are not forever bound to anything that we chose not to be. We understand our inviolate power and that we are sovereigns of ourselves. We are able to adopt a new name or to redefine ourselves and our practice especially when we recognize that it no longer serves us without the need to seek permission from anyone else. We are free to adopt a name that better conveys who we are, or a label that closer aligns with what we do, with a power that resonates better with our practice, and holds within its nature an energetic vibration that we desire to harness within.

We know and understand that, like the element of Water, we are malleable. We are able to change our etheric body, change our perspective, shift others' perception of who and what we are, and we accept only the limitations we place upon ourselves, not those inflicted upon us by others. It is with this in mind that I guide you to the following exercise.

Exercise: Defining Self

As you complete this first task, I encourage you to record the answers in your journal. The act of writing out your definitions is meaningful, the act of contemplation and recording those personal insights and feelings concerning the terms is what is important. I encourage you to record your responses and then read what you have written, allow your own words to truly manifest within your being. With this act you will solidify your own beliefs and begin reestablishing the foundation that you desire within your own practice.

Take some time to contemplate the following terms, and once you have them defined for yourself, write the word and its definition in your journal. Be sure not to use the term within its definition.

For example, do not simply define Witchcraft as *"the craft of the Witch"* without also defining both the word *craft* and the word *witch*.

- God
- Religion
- Spirituality
- Paganism
- Wicca
- Eclectic
- Priest/ess
- Witch
- Magician
- Wizard
- Sorcerer/ess
- Warlock
- Magic
- Magick
- Witchcraft
- Spell
- Prayer
- Ritual
- Charm
- Dedication
- Initiation

Chapter 2

Altered States

In most books on Witchcraft you'll find a section covering meditation. This is because meditation is a common way in which to reach an altered state of consciousness where the Witch is able to perform acts of magick. It is my belief that a Witch that is unable to reach an altered state of consciousness is a Witch who is struggling to cast a successful spell or straining to manifest a desired outcome. This is not to say that they're not casting or manifesting, but their outcomes are not exactly what they desired. This is because everything we experience in the physical begins with an idea within the mind, whether it is something we considered or a concept that someone else has thought and used to influenced us, it all begins within the intellect.

Meditation is a tool that I encourage Witches to utilize. It is a way to condition the mind and create overall health and well-being by bringing our physical body, our mind, and emotions into alignment. It is a state of conscious awareness where the mind is free of the distraction of scattered thought patterns that daily bombard the mind and is instead focused on the current state of being in the moment of meditation.

I've been often asked by my students if a Witch must meditate in the stereotypical way we most often see on the internet or in other media when we search "meditation": a Buddhist monk sitting on the floor or on a cushion with legs crossed like a pretzel, hands held palm to palm or with palms up laying on the knees, or in a mudra, and I emphatically respond: "No, not at all." While that style of meditation is certainly acceptable and will lead the Witch to achieve an altered state of consciousness, it is not the only way to meditate, and frankly, it's not usually the most successful way for the modern Witch to approach meditation at the beginning of their practice. This is due to primarily two things; the physical uncomfortability of sitting in such a pose and the bombardment of numerous distractions.

The modern American adult is accustomed to the position of sitting upright in a chair with feet on the floor. Our homes and workplaces are filled with furniture designed for this sedentary activity: armchairs, wing chairs, sofas, dining room chairs, stools, benches, desk chairs, folding chairs, and all styles of outdoor and garden seating. Sitting directly on the floor or ground is rarely encouraged after childhood. This behavior directly affects our bodies and contributes to our lack of flexibility and physical discomfort when attempting to sit in the recognizable Lotus Pose. Adopting an exercise routine that includes strength training and stretching will allow you to become more flexible and enable you to eventually achieve the beneficial Lotus Pose.

Contemporary life is full of distractions, both

desired and unwanted. We have been trained from a young age to expect constant stimulation from a variety of outside sources: our cell phones, our tablets, our computers, by music or videos, by our pets, and other people. So, for us to sit in any position in silence for an extended period of time without moving or receiving outside input, is a struggle. It is a challenge that we quickly abandon because it brings us pain. It is simply agonizing.

The expectation that can effectively shift from a modern life buzzing with movement, flashing lights, and loud noises to stillness, darkness, and silence with just one attempt is foolish. Such a drastic shift is unattainable. The momentum of our modern lives is too great to halt and reverse so quickly. I suggest that after establishing a meditation routine, you make the Buddhist style of meditation I've mentioned a goal to achieve, but not the first style you attempt.

Where should you begin if this is the first time you are establishing a practice or trying to reestablish your meditation routine? Well, there are a variety of styles and you should experiment to see which one works best for you, but to start I would suggest beginning with either a focused meditation, movement meditation, or guided meditation.

Focused meditation is the fixed concentration on a singular sound, object, or phrase. While you are focusing on either the sound, object, or phrase, you only allow your mind to dwell on that particular thing, and if other thoughts enter your mind you address them and then refocus on the chosen sound, object, or phrase.

Movement meditation is the concentration on a particular movement such as walking, running, rocking, spinning, and dancing. Yoga, T'ai chi, and

Qigong are also considered to be types of movement meditation as they bring your awareness to the positions of the body while focusing on the breath.

Guided meditation is concentrating on words spoken by another individual, usually in some type of story form, and is often partnered with music or other auditory sounds found in nature that align with the goal of the meditation. These types of meditations usually have a central theme or topic that is explored during the session.

The goal of meditation for the Witch is to gain access to the altered state of consciousness known as trance: a mental state that resembles deep sleep, where suggestibility is enhanced and the consciousness is able to disassociate from the physical body. Trance states are accessed or induced both with conscious intention and for some individuals unintentionally, not only for the purpose of working magick, but also as a way of accessing the unconscious mind for healing, relaxation, and astral travel.

As Witch our purpose is to intentionally enter a trance state to visualize the outcome of a spell, to experience that which is not yet physical, so that with our expressed Will it will become manifested in our reality. To visualize something is more than just to imagine that thing in your mind with your eyes closed, it is experiencing that which is presently non-existent, even when your eyes are opened. With successful visualization the Witch is able to see, hear, smell, taste, and feel that which she or he is creating, and because we know that everything begins within the intellect, and recognize that our mind is the most vital and powerful tool we possess, we practice the skills necessary to control our thoughts and become proficient with visualization.

Meditation has never been too difficult a challenge for me as I have sought ways in which to escape physicality since I was a child. I've had the most success with focused meditation, though at the time of this writing I have discovered that a daily movement meditation is bringing me the most over-all benefits.

A focused meditation that utilizes the sounds of binaural beats quickly and easily allows me to shift into a trance state. I use it frequently when attempting to act as the medium during seances or when doing an invocation.

Exercise: Meditation

A daily meditation practice is essential for the Witch and reestablishing a foundation for your practice would include reevaluating and adjusting your current practice if you conclude that it isn't working for you.

I urge that the Witch begin with a meditation that runs only approximately five minutes and gradually increase the length of the time for each session. If you are following a guided meditation, begin with a short and simple one, perhaps one that just encourages you to relax before attempting a longer guided meditation with a more complex goal.

You will find that some days you will struggle with focusing or letting go of your thoughts, while other days the meditation will seem easy. Don't worry, just keep a record of how you're feeling, what you've consumed (drink, food, recreational drugs, and medications), and what events occurred prior to your session; these things will influence your ability to concentrate on the meditation and will allow insight into what you may want to avoid for future sessions.

The more consistent you are with your practice, the easier it will become over time. Remember to track the results and progress of your meditation practice in your journal.

Exercise: Visualization

For this exercise you will need to gather a few objects; each should be notably different from the others in color, texture, scent, taste, and sound. Some items I suggest are: an orange (or other piece of fruit), a fork, a hair brush (or tooth brush), a set of keys, a living plant (or leaves), and a glass of wine (or tart juice).

Place the items on a table or flat surface in front of you and spend some time examining each of them. Study their appearance, manipulate each item with your hands, smell it, taste it, and listen to the sounds it is able to produce, then close your eyes and visualize each one, holding the visualization for at least five minutes.

If you find you are unable to hold it for that long, open your eyes and repeat the examination process, then close your eyes again and visualize until the five minutes have passed.

Once you are able to hold the visualization successfully for the entire five minutes, remove the items from the table and out of sight, then attempt to visualize the items with your eyes open.

When you have been successful with visualizing with open eyes, attempt to extend the time you hold the items with eyes closed, and then eyes open, eventually working towards the ability to manipulate the items within the visualization.

For example, cut the fruit and eat it, or once the fruit is cut, use the fork to eat it. Jingle the keys with your hand. Drink the glass of wine. Use the hair brush on yourself, or if you are able to visualize another individual, use it to brush their hair.

As you work with each phase of the exercise, keep a record of your successes and failures in your journal, noting any conditions within your environment or within yourself that may have influenced the outcome. As with meditation, the more consistent you are with your visualization practice, the easier it will become, and you may find that as you improve with meditation, the visualization becomes easier to achieve.

Chapter 3

The Gods

Since as far back as I can recall I have always had a relationship with deity. There was never a time I didn't believe in some greater being that was wiser than I ever could hope to be, filled with great compassion, and was all loving, even if that love wasn't expressed with a soft and gentle touch. Whether this being was the Creator of the Universe, or just some ancient presence, I have never been certain, but the simple point that it existed for me in my life has always been a piece of my spirituality that continues to exist within my own Witchcraft.

I am aware that atheists exist and that they are not phantoms, but real people with whom I have come in contact. I can mentally reason as to the "why" of their belief, but I do struggle with embracing the complete understanding of it. It is personally difficult for me to believe that there isn't anything more or anything more beyond humanity as we currently experience it in our physical bodies in this life. How can any human being disregard the possibility of the existence of a collective consciousness? While we are living in physicality, we are limited by it. We are restricted by the vessel that is required to experience human life.

Frankly I have a much easier time understanding individuals who hold an agnostic point of view because I have experienced spans of transition in my own life when I had lost faith in God and had been unable to see just how I was going to thrive and continue to live, but I knew that even dwelling in that darkness there was something beyond, I just didn't have a name or label for it.

I have met Witches who consciously separate their Craft from their spirituality, and I have met Witches who meld the two effortlessly. I can certainly understand both perspectives. Personally, I have always been spiritual in nature, and regardless of what religion I followed or spirituality I resonated with, my practices have always been a major part of my life, and it is no different with my Craft. Since the moment I began studying magick I have always perceived it to be a part of my spiritual practice, but I don't necessarily believe it *must* be. It doesn't matter if I don't understand how an individual is able to separate their spirituality from Witchcraft, because my comprehension of it doesn't mean it cannot be done successfully.

Getting *"back to the basics"* and solidifying your foundation within your Craft includes a reevaluation of your beliefs concerning deity. Understanding how you perceive this concept will enable you to achieve your best results within your Witchcraft, even if your belief is that deity doesn't truly exist as a supreme spiritual entity, but is instead a psychological archetype or thoughtform or something else entirely. Your belief is valid and true regardless of what other

Witches, including myself, believe about your understanding or personal gnosis concerning the gods. Remember, you are the sovereign of your Craft. You hold inviolate personal power and identifying where this originates within you will enable you to be a successful Witch who creates her or his own reality.

Who or what deity is, how they or it influences your life, and what type of relationship you have with them or it, will be key points for you to contemplate. Many individuals, not just Witches, possess a belief in the existence of a supreme power or primordial force, whether it is a personified deity or a formless web of energy, there is a consensus that it influences every aspect of life on the planet. Some perceive the nature of deity to be immanent, within all of creation, and some perceive it to be transcendent, outside or beyond the scope of creation, while still others perceive it to be both and manifested through all of physical creation.

My personal perception of deity has shifted over the years through my own becoming as Witch from a monotheistic belief, (when I was Christian), to a duotheistic belief, (when I was Wiccan), to a polytheistic belief, (before my transition), to my current perception of deity; a less personified view and more expansive in nature, though I still observe and understand there is an existence of a spiritual force that is greater than myself, which energetically connects all living beings. I do not work with a particular deity or pantheon, instead I embrace this ethereal force in its expressed polarity of masculine and feminine energies and refer to such as the primordial feminine and primordial masculine forces of the Universe.

Matron and Patron Gods

It isn't unusual for a polytheistic Witch to exclusively work with and worship one specific goddess or god, or a complimentary pair, commonly referred to as their Matron and Patron respectively. This intimate relationship is cultivated over time through meditation, contemplation, divination, ritual, and magickal workings. While this practice isn't uncommon, it isn't a necessary relationship to have and cultivate with the gods. At the time of this writing, I do not have such a relationship and my Craft is not the least bit lacking in depth or sacredness.

There are two different perspectives when it comes to the concept of Matron and Patron gods. The first perspective is that the gods, because of the nature of their being, do not choose a specific Witch as they have no need for worship or communion with human beings. The gods are accessible to all, but the Witch must achieve a level of enlightenment in order to perceive them and the nature of who and what they are in their purest form. From this perspective the Witch chooses the particular Matron or Patron they desire to know or to worship or to show devotion, and begins the relationship with that specific goddess or god.

The second perspective is that a specific god called the Witch because the Witch has a need that can be fulfilled by the god through worship or communion with this particular divine energy. From this perspective the god chooses the Witch, who in turn will worship, devote their Craft, and learn from the god as the relationship is formed and nurtured over time.

Regardless of the perspective you hold, personal gnosis is key to discovering what goddess or god is most beneficial for your personal growth. There are numerous tools available for you to use as you seek to uncover which goddess or god is calling you or would best suit you. The aids that I have found to be most helpful are: dreams, divination, meditation, introspection, prayer, spells, and research. I would be remiss if I didn't mention that the identity of a Matron or Patron god is revealed differently to each Witch and greatly depends on the style of Witchcraft you practice. Usually there are signs indicating which god you are best aligned with or who is calling you, but it is common to miss many of them as they occur; in hindsight, however, they tend to be glaringly obvious.

For example, ObsidianFire's intuition indicates that she is ready for a Matron goddess in her Craft. She does a simple spell on Friday's full Moon with the intention: "reveal my Matron". Within days of casting the spell her friend asks if she would care for her dog, Odin, while she went out of town on business. A month later, she goes on holiday to Sweden, and whenever she did a Tarot reading for herself concerning the topic of a Matron, The Empress card would appear in the layout. She experienced reoccurring dreams about spinning thread and frequently she would discover that a stray goat had found its way into her garden. But the most prominent sign for her was when she received a friend request on social media from someone named Freya. While each of these signs didn't really point her in a direction on their own, when she compiled them together it was clear to see that Frigga / Freya was the goddess being indicated.

Exercise: Questions Concerning Deity

In this exercise I encourage you to take some time to contemplate the following questions regarding the overall concept of deity. Allow your thoughts to wander where they may as you record your responses in your journal.

1. Do you view deity as immanent or transcendent?
2. In what ways does deity manifest on Earth, if at all?
3. What do you believe is the most important thing for you to understand about the nature of deity?
4. Is the Universe meaningless or do you believe it holds a meaningful structure?
5. Do you believe in the existence of personified deities, or do you perceive it as a formless energy?

The following questions are for those who work with personified deity:

6. Do you believe that the gods created human beings, or that human beings created the gods?
7. How much influence do you believe the gods have over the physical realm?
8. Do you believe that the gods have a purpose? Is there an agenda? If so, what do you believe this purpose is and what part do you play in that purpose?
9. What attributes and characteristics do you associate with the gods?
10. In what ways are you developing and nurturing a relationship with the gods? With your Matron or Patron?

Exercise: Relationship with Deity

Take some time to contemplate the following common classifications given to the numerous beliefs regarding deity. Once you have determined your own perception of deity, write the classification with its definition in your journal along with your own thoughts and feelings regarding the concept of deity.

- Duotheism: the belief that there are only

two gods of equal power.
- Pantheism: the belief that all is god.
- Panentheism: the belief that god exists within everything.
- Polytheism: the belief that there are many gods, usually assembled in a pantheon.
    - Hard Polytheism: the belief that all gods are distinct and separate.
    - Soft Polytheism: the belief that all gods are part of one god.
- Henotheism: the acceptance of the existence or possible existence of many gods, but only believing that one god is supreme.
- Kathenotheism: the acceptance of the existence of many gods, but worshiping only one god at a time.
- Monotheism: the belief that there is one god that exists and all other gods are misunderstandings or aspects of that one god.

Chapter 4

Magick

Getting "*back to the basics*" means covering all the rudimentary concepts within Witchcraft that we learned early within our practice. Magick is not only one of the key concepts, but a vital one to understand. I have always resonated with Aleister Crowley's definition of magick: "*the Science and Art of causing Change to occur in conformity with Will*", but over the years I have rewritten it to incorporate my own personal understandings of the concept of magick and now define it as: "*the art of manipulating Will, emotions, and energy, in order to bring about change within an individual's reality, whether it is outside or within.*" While my definition is based on Crowley's, I acknowledge that emotions play a role in the manipulation of energy when it comes to magick, which is most likely due to the influence of the teachings of Abraham-Hicks on my own Craft. Regardless of how you define magick, there is no denying that it imbues everything. It is the interconnection of energy that binds all reality, which is the reason that we, as Witches, are able to manifest our desired outcome into physical reality. We tap into the interconnectedness through our skills with visualization and harness the energy in order to manipulate it and bring our desired change from the nonphysical Unseen Realms into the physical.

We recognize that because we are all bound by this magickal energy, we are never separate from it, and in essence we are just a small part of the whole. We are as connected to our biological mother as we are connected to the tree in our front yard or the smallest protozoan in the vastness of the ocean, and it is this connection which allows us to work magick for or on a target that is beyond our physical reach. The distance between us doesn't matter because we are extensions of this vast web of energy.

The energy that imbues our corporeal body is a facet of who we are and is flavored by our personality, giving each of us a distinct vibrational signature, which can be read by psychics and other Witches. It is in part what distinguishes ObsidianFire and her Witchcraft from CricketSong and her magickal workings. While experiencing physical life, all parts of our body: the cells, tissue, bones, organs, secretions, and all waste it produces, contain our energy until that energy transfers elsewhere or diminishes over time.

If we have in our possession a part of an individual's body, like a stand of hair or drops of blood, then we in essence possess a part of that person; a small part of them is the same as having the totality of them. This concept includes possessing an item that the individual owns or something they wore or used often, like a piece of jewelry or a favorite tee shirt. Using these items enables the Witch to manipulate the energies of the individual easier and with a greater opportunity for success when doing a magickal working or casting a spell, regardless whether it's for a benevolent or malicious purpose.

If it's impossible to obtain a part of the target's body or an item that he or she owns, then utilizing a photo or avatar of the target will work just as well. When there is a physical resemblance between target and image there exists an energetic alignment that is easily manipulated by the Witch. For example, if my friend, who lives in France, is unable to be with me in person for a healing spell that I plan to cast for her, it would be prudent to print a photograph of her from facebook and use that in her place, or an even a better option would be to craft a poppet and attach the photograph of her. All magick done to this poppet would then be done to her due to the energetic alignment between the two because of the physical resemblance.

The Witches' Pyramid

The Witches' Pyramid is a philosophy within Witchcraft that was first written about by the French occultist Eliphas Levi in his book, titled *Transcendental Magic: Its Doctrine and Ritual*, and defines how magick can be successfully employed by aligning with the four powers: To Know, To Dare, To Will, and To Keep Silence. The addition of the fifth power, To Go, is accredited to magician Aleister Crowley, who in his work, *The Book of Thoth*, introduced the purpose of the inclusion. Crowley was greatly influenced by the teachings of Levi and the addition of this newer fifth power is what marks the distinction between Levi's teachings of *The Four Powers of the Magus or Sphinx* and the modern teaching of *The Witches' Pyramid*.

Many books written about the topic of magick and Witchcraft include a section about *The Witches' Pyramid* and I would be remiss to neglect it this book that focuses on getting "*back to the basics*" of the Craft. I not only practice the concepts presented within *The Witches' Pyramid* in my own Craft, I view them as vital bricks in any strong magickal foundation.

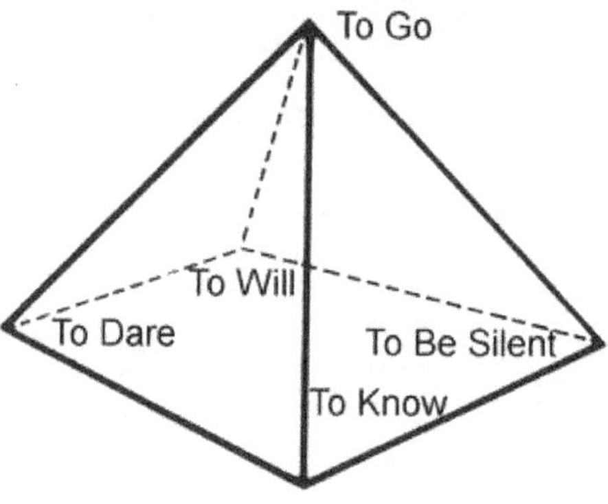

The first side of the pyramid is To Know, which addresses accumulative knowledge; the seeking, gathering, and consumption of all information, as well as the thorough understanding of the data. The information would include, but is not limited to, book knowledge. It should also include the familiarity of oneself, the strengths and weaknesses possessed by the Witch or magickal practitioner, the natural talents and learned skills, the assertions and fears she or he holds, and any other information that is able to be uncovered. Personal observations concerning: people, animals, nature, the gods, spirits, the physical world, and the Unseen Realms beyond, are included in the gathering and understanding of To Know.

This power includes the Witch's awareness that all human beings are constantly influenced by outside stimulus, whether if at the time of this influence we are conscious of it or not, and that as Witch, with diligence, we evaluate our personal motives before we take action, both magickal and mundane. We consider the energies of planetary alignment and other astrological occurrences that may be influencing us, the Seasonal Tides, other living people, spiritual entities, and the thoughtforms that we encounter on a daily basis.

These mental constructs that are energetically birthed into existence by human beings, either consciously or unconsciously, have independent existence in the Astral Realm and influence on the Physical Realm for as long as they are fed. The extent of a thoughtform's influence directly corresponds to the number of people and the force of human emotional energy being channeled to it. Minor thoughtforms, such as the harmony of a home, will only influence those who reside in the home or who visit, while in comparison a more substantial and influential thoughtform, such as patriotism, will affect a greater population and encompass a larger area. The Witch mastering the first power of The Witches' Pyramid would be able to distinguish between her or his own thoughts and beliefs and those that are manipulating them.

The power of To Know encompasses the Witch's willingness to change a currently held perception when it no longer serves a personal truth. Seeking knowledge never ends; it is part of the process of becoming Witch and will continue throughout your lifetime.

The second side of the pyramid is To Dare; this

power is the ability to overcome fear and insecurity with confidence gained through the accumulated knowledge and the abilities, and the skills that have been learned, in order to be proactive in acts of magick and Witchcraft. To cast a spell or to attempt to do a magickal working involves a level of risk that not all are willing to take. There are no guarantees in life or magick, but the Witch understands that it takes courage to act on that which she or he has committed themselves to, regardless of whether or not they possess previous experience in which to draw upon.

A Witch understands and trusts their instincts and intuition when dealing with the unknown, whether it is worldly and mundane or otherworldly and magickal in nature. Walking into unfamiliar territory, traversing the Unseen Realms, or exploring the darkness within; all require daring, the willingness to confront whatever might be lurking in wait. Not all individuals are born to become Witch and not all are meant to be. It takes a unique individual to wear the pointed hat; someone courageous, unafraid of living outside of normality, an outcast, a misfit, a weirdo, a freak. Someone who doesn't really fit in with the rest of society and finds comfort in solitude, someone who is willing to unapologetically confront whatever obstacles they encounter, if when they are the only one who is able to see it.

The third side of the pyramid is To Will, which works in tandem with To Dare. To Will is the force of the Witch's concentrated intention put into action. It is an expression of the purest desire and is used by the Witch to express a command. It is synonymous with determination, insistence, and persistence; all of which are vital to the manifestation of a spell or magickal working.

Will with the capital letter W speaks to the idea of purpose, a concept that can be found within the beliefs of numerous spiritual paths. It is the reason for manifesting in physicality, and ultimately the Witch's life's purpose. Aleister Crowley wrote about the idea of True Will and defined it as: *"an individual's grand destiny in life"*. If the Witch follows her or his True Will, then that individual would be in perfect alignment with Nature. These actions would not be sparked by conscious intent, but instead would be the interplay between the deepest Self and the Universe and therefore would direct the Witch towards her or his destiny, their personal motivation for manifesting on the planet.

Crowley's philosophy was greatly influenced by the idea of the True Self discussed in the writings of Éliphas Lévi and the philosophical and esoteric tradition of Hermeticism. The individuals who follow this school of ideas seek to reunite the split nature of all human beings, thus freeing the True Self, which is enslaved to the desires and physicality of the body. It is through this effort or Great Work that humanity is returned to a state of unity with the Universe, but it must be done through gnosis. Following the True Self, which is the part of the Universe or Divinity that was separated, would lead the Witch to actions that are absent of conscious intention, and are instead guided by The All.

Will can also be linked to the belief of geas found within Irish and Welsh mythology, which can be compared to a curse or being held to a vow or oath, that if broken leads to overwhelmingly disastrous consequences, but when observed leads the Witch to great power as she or he would be thusly behaving in order with the intention of that which was predetermined at birth.

These three concepts of True Will, True Self, and geas are only a few examples of how many religions, philosophies, and spiritual paths perceive the understanding of Will, the untainted and purest desire of the Witch. The vehicle in which this power is manifested into our shared reality is visualization, and without the power To Will there would be no reason To Dare.

The last side of the pyramid is the power To Be Silent. Silence is the absence of sound and noise, which is a rarity in today's modern society as we are constantly bombarded by clamor and babble, but silence is required by the Witch as it is the bridge between what is seen and unseen, that which is known and unknown, what is and what is yet to be realized. Silence is therefore understood to be a Witch's greatest ally. Within silence new concepts and ideas are learned and clear communication between the Witch's conscious and unconscious is achieved, allowing the mind, without the necessity to filter out extraneous noise, to contemplate and integrate all new information that is gained through research, study, and experimentation, or through experience.

As the Witch recognizes that all words hold a vibration that can affect those who read or hear the word when it is spoken, and that not all words are equal in this power, we know how important it is to "think before we speak". To use the power of To Be Silent in this way allows us to choose the words we utter with care, understanding that often the connotation of our words or the way in which we speak them, our tone and volume, has the ability to shift the power of them.

Knowing which words to use, which words to avoid, and when not to speak at all, requires insight gained from life experience. Just because you are knowledgeable about Witchcraft or magick doesn't mean that you are required to share that knowledge with others even when they ask it of you. Sometimes in some circumstances, it is best to remain silent and allow others to learn through their own study and experience.

It benefits the Witch to prepare for all magickal workings and spell castings within the cloak of silence, as it allows time for contemplation and for the whisperings of our inner voice to reach us, bringing the helpful guidance we may require. When we share our magickal plans with others, we solicit judgement and criticism, which may lead to direct interference and resistance to our intention, the greatest of which typically manifests as self-doubt. Silence is the tool of untainted intent.

Once all four powers are mastered, the energies gather and propel the intention towards manifestation, this is the power of To Go. Aleister Crowley wrote about the special relationship between the four powers discussed by Elphias Levi: To Know, To Will, To Dare, To Keep Silence, and his addition of the fifth power To Go within his work, *The Book of Thoth*:

"... the names of the four Virtues of the Adept, those which enable him to overcome the resistance of the elements; they are: to Will, to Dare, to Know and to Keep Silence. By the harmonious exercise of these, the fifth Element of Spirit is formulated in the being of the Adept. It is the god within, the sun, which is the centre of the Universe from the human point of view,

with its own particular virtue, which is to Go. The essential characteristic of the godhead is this faculty of Going; the free movements of space and time and all other possible conditions."

To Go is the power of the moment when the Witch has integrated the four powers of the pyramid and is ready to act upon her or his desire. The Witch has gathered the required knowledge and possesses a willingness to courageously confront any resistance that may be encountered while working the magick to create the changes desired within their reality.

The Witches' Pyramid works together with one power triggering the next; in order To Dare the Witch must (To) Know; in order To Will the Witch must (To) Dare; the Witch must (To) Will to create their intention; and to hold the manifestation the Witch must (To) Be Silent.

Time and Space

As a human being, you perceive your life in a linear fashion. You use this structure to organize and make sense of the experiences you encounter during your lifetime in the Physical Realm, but time is a manmade construct. It is an observed phenomenon by means of which we sense and record changes in our environment and in the universe. While a literal definition of time is as elusive as time itself, it has been called an illusion, a dimension, a smooth-flowing continuum, and an expression of separation among events that occur in the same physical location, which is defined as space.

Space is experienced by most human beings as occurring all at once. As you walk into a room, you simultaneously view the totality of the room, but if you were blindfolded, as you entered through the doorway, you would experience the space in a linear fashion. After colliding into the first piece of furniture, you would use your sense of touch, smell, sound, and perhaps taste, to determine what it was you bumped into and where it was located in the room, then after moving forward you would slam into the next item located in the area, and then the next, and the next, until you had explored the entirety of the room. Your brain would organize the space in the same linear fashion as you had experienced it, just as it organizes time; each item in the room is understood as a life experience or a moment of your lifetime.

The human brain is unable to comprehend the idea that time occurs all at once because it perceives it in a straight line, but the reality is that time is not linear. The linear concept is simply a tool and as such it is not something that governs or controls the Witch. It is a creation that human beings have made for their benefit, to structure and make sense of life.

Time is malleable and therefore not an absolute, and the Witch recognizes the power this implies. All magickal workings and cast spells effect a change in a future that simply does not exist. Magick is the manipulation of energy that is currently present in order to shift the perception of the target so that the change that has been made can be perceived in the present moment, and establishing sacred space or casting Circle is creating a "place between the realms", which supersedes both the time and space illusions. The ability to perceive an event that exists in the linear future, but is in actuality a part of the simultaneous now is the psychic ability we label clairvoyance or "clearly seeing", and the ability to recollect a past-life is perceiving a simultaneous life experience. Embracing and understanding this knowledge concerning the manmade constructs of time and how the human brain structures space, grants the Witch a greater perspective of our shared reality and enables her or him to manipulate the energies and illusions to create a desired change.

Exercise: Candle Flame

In the simplest terms, magick is the manipulation of energy, and as Witch you have been using magick with some success to manifest change in your life. *Getting back to the basics* means revisiting your Craft and the ways and reasons you are practicing it.

For this exercise you will need a candle, (a taper candle works best), a candle holder, a match or lighter to light the candle, and a quiet place where you will not be disturbed.

Place the candle in the candle holder and set the holder on a table in front of you at a comfortable height so that when you rest your hands on the table you are not straining. Rest your hands palms down on the table on either side of the candle.

At this point I encourage you to read through the

rest of this exercise.

After reading the following steps, return to this point and visualize yourself completing the exercise with success. Take time with the visualization, allowing it to unfold in real time. If you are able to visualize with your eyes open, do so as this is the preferred method.

At the conclusion of your visualization, proceed with the exercise and light the candle. Allow the flame to burn for a few moments while you gaze at it.

While focusing on the burning flame, rub your palms together to build up the energy in your hands. Slowly extend your hands towards the candle with palms on either side of the flame, close enough to feel the heat, but far enough away to not burn your skin.

As you focus on the flame extend your energy towards the flame and gently pull the flame closer to the palm of your dominate hand. Hold the flame there for a few minutes.

Release your energetic hold on the flame, then switch palms and pull the candle flame closer to the palm of your non-dominate hand. Hold it there for a few minutes then release your hold on the flame.

Repeat the exercise in its entirety, extending the time you hold the flame with each palm.

Remember to record the results of the exercise and any insights you have in your journal. Be sure to note any conditions within your environment or within yourself that may have influenced the outcome.

Exercise: Energy Ball

This exercise isn't new, but rather a staple energy exercise that can be found in many different practices around the globe. You will be creating a ball of energy through visualization.

First you should give your personal energy a color. There is not "right" or "wrong" choice with this, but it should hold personal meaning for you.

Once you have determined the color of your energy, you will determine the size of the energy ball you will be creating. If this is your first attempt at this type of exercise, the ideal size would be that of a grapefruit.

At this point I encourage you to read through the rest of this exercise as you did with the previous one.

After reading the entirety of the exercise, return to this point and visualize yourself completing it successfully. Take time with the visualization, allowing it to unfold in real time. If you are able to visualize with your eyes opened, do so as this is the preferred method.

At the conclusion of your visualization, proceed with the exercise and rub your hands together briskly a few times to build up the energy in your palms.

Extend your hands holding them about three inches apart and palm to palm as if you were going to clap them together. Concentrate on the sensations you feel on your palms as you feel the energy gathering.

Slowly move your palms apart a few inches then just as slowly bring them back towards each other so that they are about three inches apart once more.

Hold them here for a few moments. Again, focus your attention to the sensations you experience between your hands as you feel the energy accumulating.

Again, slowly move your hands apart a few inches and slowly bring them back to their original position.

Repeat this process until you feel some resistance as you try to return your palms to their original position of about three inches apart. When you feel that resistance – do not push passed it. This distance now becomes your new starting position.

Slowly move your palms apart a few inches then just as slowly bring them back towards each other, stopping at your new starting position.

Repeat the process of expanding and condensing the energy ball between your palms until it has reached the approximate size you determined at the beginning of the exercise.

When you are satisfied with the size of your energy ball, shift it so that you are holding it in your dominate or projective hand.

Push the energy ball into the ground or floor where it will be reabsorbed and redistributed into the planet. If you are familiar with this exercise and wish to gift your ball of energy to someone or something, or want to reabsorb the energy back into yourself, then you should do so.

Remember to record the results of the exercise in your journal. Note any conditions within your environment or within yourself that may have influenced the outcome.

Consider how your energy within the ball felt; was it hot, cold, sharp, smooth? Did it tingle? What insights did you gain about your personal energy?

Exercise: Energy Ball Revisited

Do not attempt this exercise until you have successfully completed the previous exercise, *Exercise: Energy Ball.*

To begin this exercise, you will create an energy ball as you did in the previous exercise.

Concentrate on holding the energy ball in your non-dominate hand, which is your receptive hand. When you have a firm visualization of this, allow the ball of energy to gradually seep into your palm so that it permeates your hand.

Now very slowly move the ball of energy up through your wrist and into your forearm. Do not rush this experience.

Continue to ease the ball along your upper arm, through your shoulder and into your chest, where you should pause the movement of the energy ball.

If you are a Witch, who works with the esoteric Indian belief of the chakras or psychic energy centers, allow the energy ball to merge with your Heart chakra. Feel the sensation of the energy permeating your chakras as it flows from your Heart Center.

Take your time with this entire exercise. Be sure you are proceeding at a very slow pace as you concentrate on the movement of the energy ball. Moving the ball too quickly or hastily will fragment your focus and the ball will dissipate within your body. If this does occur, you should restart the exercise from the beginning.

Once you have merged the energy ball with your Heart Center, or have spent time feeling the energy saturate your chest, continue to carefully move it over to the opposite shoulder, then direct it down your upper arm, slowly along your forearm, down to your wrist, and into your opposite hand.

When the ball of energy is in your hand, allow it to gradually seep out of your body as when you allowed it to seep into your body at the beginning of the exercise.

Gather the energy ball in the palm of your dominate hand. The energy should feel different from when you began the exercise. It should feel denser, more compressed and empowered from its journey through your body, having spent time within your Heart Center or chest.

When you have successfully moved the energy ball from your receptive hand to your projective hand, your nondominated hand to your dominate hand, you can return the energy to the earth, or your own body, or gift it to someone or something that might benefit from a boost in energy.

Remember to record the results of the exercise in your journal, making note of any conditions within your environment or within yourself that may have influenced a successful outcome.

Consider how the energy ball felt:

- At the beginning of the exercise, did the energy ball feel hot, cold, sharp, soft, hard, smooth? Did it tingle or burn?
- As the energy ball traveled through your body, how did it feel? Was there a transition of sensations when it lingered in your chest, in your Heart Center?
- At the conclusion of the exercise, did the energy ball feel the same as when you began? Did it still feel hot, cold, sharp, soft, hard, smooth? Did it still tingle or burn?
- If you gifted your energy to someone, did they comment on how it felt to them? What was the results of your gifting the energy ball?
- What insights did you gain about your personal energy by doing the exercise?

Chapter 5

Witch's Honor

As we journey to becoming Witch and get *back to the basics* of our Witchcraft, reevaluating and restating our principles and morals is an important step in establishing a strong magickal foundation.

Our principles, the behaviors that govern how we live our lives and how we work our magick, change over the course of our lifetime. They are the foundation of who we are, Witch or cowan, and are shaped by life experiences both magickal and mundane as we interact with the energies of people, places, and events that occur during our lifetime.

As Witch we gain wisdom and insight through our Craft; the spiritual encounters we experience, the spells we cast, the magickal workings we undertake. These activities shape our basic principles and moral code of behavior, which are motivators as to what magickal workings and spells a Witch will do or will not cast.

Morals define our overall character and are typically unchanging unless we experience a defining moment such as a serious trauma or near-death experience. Our moral code defines what behaviors we view as virtuous and what deeds we understand to be profane. Within society we have agreed as a collective on a moral code. For example, committing wicked acts such as murder, will ultimately result in the perpetrator receiving a punishment, while engaging in virtuous acts the individual, recognized as a hero, will gain a reward or recognition by others within our society.

It is prudent for the Witch to understand that even though many of your morals may be universal, as they are often based in common human emotional experiences, others can vary from Witch to Witch. We all have a different past, have lived different lives, and these past experiences will shape our principles and morals. Not all Witches adhere to the Wiccan principle of, *"An it harm none, do as you will"*, but most of us know when we've crossed the line; we know when we've done something that is wrong or against our own sense of honor. The Witch claims responsibility for her or his actions and isn't quick to blame another person or spiritual entity for the questionable behavior. We accept the consequences of what we say and do mundanely and magickally.

A Witch's honor is built over time as she or he experiences life, makes both big and small decisions that reflect the quality of their character, what ideals, principles, and morals she or he adopts. It's based on the integrity of the Witch and whether they are seeking to advance themselves and their Craft or are experiencing personal erosion, neither condition is morally good or bad in and of itself, but would be qualified as such by the Witch themselves. Just as the tides ebb and flow, so does the Witch's personal experience within their Craft. There is a time for expansion and a time for attrition; both are beneficial, both are required for overall development.

When the Witch improves her or himself, they better the condition of all else as each of us are simply an extension of the eternal energy that permeates everything in existence; just as when we better the condition of all else, we in turn improve ourselves. The simplest thing we can do to improve the quality of all life on our planet is to use our unique understanding and ability to wield magick to aid and support the local ecology in whatever means we have available to us. It is important to understand that even these acts, though holding a unified intention, may look different from Witch to Witch as we each practice Witchcraft in different ways.

It is magick that binds all reality, the unseen fundamental energy, which is comparable to electricity in the way it can be used, and just as an electrical current holds no color, neither does magick. An electrical current does hold a charge similar to an intention held within a magickal working or spell. The electrical current itself is neither righteous nor wicked, but is solely dependent on the way in which the individual will use the electricity. The individual's purpose may be viewed by others or even themselves as virtuous or corrupt, but electricity itself has no quantifiable moral value. The same can be said of magick.

Magick itself is neither righteous nor wicked, neither white nor black, but is solely dependent on the intention and Will of the Witch who wields it. It is the Witch's intention that may be viewed by others or even the Witch her or himself as benevolent or malevolent, but magick itself has no quantifiable moral value. Magick is energy, the energy that binds everything into our shared physical reality and is manipulated along with Will and emotions in order to bring about change within reality.

Just as electricity takes the path of least resistance, the same holds true of magick, both are expressions of energy and any attempt to move through channels that are contrary or hold conflicting vibrations will require more effort and power to be expended. The path of the least resistance is the most easily accessible and is the most desirable.

While it may not be a popular point to discuss, and many individuals will take offense to this next suggestion, it is one that I believe is important to consider. Since magick takes the path of least resistance, and the Witch, possessing both body and mind, is a channel for energy, it is logical to conclude that a Witch in the state of health and overall well-being will be able to use magick more efficiently and will witness the manifestations of their spell castings and magickal workings quicker than the Witch who is not.

Struggling with a physical ailment, emotional distress, or mental illness will create resistance within the Witch. This does not mean that if you are dealing with such issues you are unable to work your Craft successfully, it simply implies that when doing so, you will be required to put forth more effort, and more power in order to be successful. This understanding of the nature of energy and the way in which magick works is why many Witches encourage self-care by promoting such practices as eating healthy, getting enough rest, exercising in some form, meditating and finding ways in which to focus the mind, unplugging from social media, setting personal boundaries, connecting with Nature, and living off-grid.

The path of least resistance is a path of willingness and a desire to comply, even if never vocalized. If the Witch attempts to cast a spell upon an individual who believes in the existence and power of magick, then there is a willingness to accept the manifestation of the desired outcome, which in comparison to an individual who believes that magick only exists in the imaginary world of fairy tales and make-believe, holds a greater possibility of a perceived manifestation. The cast spell in turn has a greater success rate with the first individual than the second because magick will always take the path of least resistance.

Willingness is a state of being that is easier for energy to transverse than the state of disbelief. Seeking consent from a target increases the chance of our cast spell or magickal working manifesting because of the target's disposition to perceive and accept the outcome. While there is a common belief that a Witch should always gain consent before casting a spell or doing a magickal working on or for the benefit of another, all morals and principles aside, it is not necessary. Consent aids the Witch's magick, it makes the process easier, requiring less effort and power from the Witch for the manifestation to occur.

When the Witch uses magick against someone or casts a spell to control or manipulate another person's actions in a way that is in direct opposition to the individual's vocalized desire, it will take more energy, more effort, more power from the Witch to manifest this change than if she or he had first gained consent.

Some would argue that in manipulating another person's energy, the Witch is altering the course of that individual's life, and while I agree that no one can truly determine the best decision to make or the best course of action to take except that individual, sometimes that person may be unable to make the decision, leaving the responsibility to someone else. At other times it may be desired or even warranted for the benefit of "the greater good" to not only make an uncomfortable decision, but to enforce that course of action even if it is a choice the individual may not have made for themselves.

But let's not be foolish here, not every Witch is motivated by altruism. Not every spell cast or every magickal working done is for the benefit of all of humanity. Many times the Witch will cast a spell or do a magickal working for her or his own benefit, which is perfectly acceptable. Personal gain is not an issue here, we don't live in the fantasy world of *Charmed*, where there is the unyielding threat of suffering unwanted consequences ranging from losing the gained benefit to death when we use our magick for our own benefit. Frankly, I believe that a Witch who cannot cast for her or his own self really has no business casting for others. If the Witch is unable to manifest a desired change in their own life, then why would anyone else trust that they had the skill, knowledge, or wisdom to do so for someone else?

This does not mean that I should not do the mundane work required to change my reality, nor should I stop encouraging others to do the work for themselves, but that there are always consequences to our actions and we are solely responsible for them. Whether it was Peter Parker who stated it first or the French Enlightenment writer, Voltaire, it still remains a truth recognized by many that "*with great power comes great responsibility*", and sometimes because I can do something, I should, and at other times, I shouldn't. Our world is such a complex place with so many different intentions, desires, and agendas swirling in the ethers around us, that no one set of rules, morals, or laws fit every circumstance, and the person that says there is, is naïve. You, as Witch, may be called to act when others simply cannot.

The Witch should therefore consider the concept of equivalent exchange, the idea that absolutely everything has a price and that nothing is given freely. Absolutely nothing. This does not suggest that the value of everything in life is easily perceived, but that everything possesses a value, and if something is desired then something of at least equal value must be given in exchange for it. Just as energy is never created, it is just transformed or shifted from one thing or place to another, so is magick since it is an expression of energy. The price or exchange may be something that is easily understood, accepted, and expected, or something that is not recognized, not conceded to, and wasn't imagined, which is the reason why it is best to contemplate any spell casting or magickal working before it is practically done.

The idea of Equivalent Exchange is akin to what is commonly known as The Law of Return, an explanation for the effect of our magickal workings, which states that for every action we take there is an equal and opposite reaction occurring even when we are not privy to what it is, where it is occurring, or when it is happening. This concept does not incorporate or even suggest a hint of morality; it is purely scientific in nature. Sir Isaac Newton's Third Law of Motion states:

"When one body exerts a force on a second body, the second body simultaneously exerts a force equal in magnitude and opposite in direction to that of the first body."

Whatever magickal working or spell the Witch casts, an equal and opposite reaction will be returned. This doesn't suggest that if the Witch does a healing spell then she or he will be cursed, not at all, what it means is that the Witch should expect that there will be a consequence equal to the power that was infused in their magickal working or spell that will manifest in that Witch's life. For a mundane example, if I push a swinging door open, that door will swing back at me with the same force I used and would have the potential of whacking me right in the face. And for a magickal example, if I cast a spell to heal a sick child, that healing energy will return to me with the same force or momentum I used and would have the potential of healing me of illness as well.

Understanding that our actions have a direct effect on others, even if we are ignorant of what that effect might be or where it may occur, cultivates a sense of personal accountability and encourages the Witch to acknowledge the active force we are, within the construct of our shared reality. Witches have a unique responsibility, unlike those who disbelieve the existence and the influential power of magick.

Does all this information therefore imply that a Witch can not curse or use baneful magick, that Witches must only cast healing spells and be altruistic with their magickal workings? Absolutely not! There is no commandment or rule dictating the behavior of Witches. This information gives the Witch awareness of the scientific concept of the nature of energy and prepares the Witch for possible consequences of her or his magick. It is most beneficial for the Witch to have protection or wards in place before throwing a curse as there will always be the returning force to the cast spell or magickal working regardless of whether or not you desire that energy or are prepared for it.

Personally, I don't blindly throw curses at individuals who have betrayed me, nor do I hastily work a malediction on those who have wronged me, because I understand the implication of Newton's observations. I understand that the individual who has taken it upon themselves to send the negative energy and possibility harmful intention towards me, in whatever form they have chosen, will experience that same energy returning to them in accordance with the Third Law of Motion. There is nothing I am required to do because they will most likely experience it through their own actions. I witness enough ugliness and negativity in the world that I don't add to the vibration, if it isn't necessary. But just because I don't enjoy it, doesn't mean I won't, if I deem it necessary.

Exercise: Random Acts of Kindness

This exercise was designed for the Witch to experience a return of energy that was intentionally given to others. Since it is beneficial for the Witch to receive kindness, kindness must be sent forth.

It is best if this exercise is practiced for approximately one lunar cycle, though you may experience results sooner depending on the effort you invest and the momentum of energy you build.

Choose from the provided list or choose an action you've determined for yourself that is aligned with the intention of kindness and fulfill it. Be sure to visualize the outcome before you act so that your intention is propelled towards the target and manifested.

Be sure to track your results and progress with this exercise in your journal, noting any "blessings" or positive experiences that happen to you while you are engaged in this exercise. Remember that there are no coincidences when working magick – it is all a result of your workings.

List of Acts of Kindness:
- Give a compliment.

- Write a letter of appreciation.
- Write letters to soldiers overseas.
- Leave anonymous inspirational notes for others to find.
- Bring flowers to someone living in a nursing home or staying in a hospital.
- Pick up litter.
- Allow someone to go before you in line.
- Hold the door open for someone.
- Help someone with bags or packages.
- Mow a neighbor's lawn.
- Rake leaves in a neighbor's yard.
- Shovel snow for an elderly neighbor.
- Walk a neighbor's dog.
- Babysit for a friend.
- Housesit for someone.
- Volunteer at a charity or non-profit organization such as: a local animal rescue or shelter, a soup kitchen or food pantry, your public library, Big Brothers Big Sisters of America, Habitat for Humanity, United Way.
- Offer to clean a friend's home.
- Help a friend move before you're asked.
- Offer to read books to children at a daycare center, preschool, or library.
- Tutor someone.
- Leave water bottles out for waste collectors, mail delivery workers, or other delivery people on a hot day.
- Pay for someone's coffee or tea.
- Donate a bag of groceries to a food pantry.

- Adopt a highway.
- Donate blood to American Red Cross.
- Donate new or used clothing to Women's Centers, Homeless Shelters, or church thrift shops.
- Plant a community garden.
- Establish a little free library.
- Leave a larger tip than usual to your waiter.

Chapter 6

Familiar and Unfamiliar Spirits

Reviewing your beliefs regarding spiritual entities and evaluating those relationships that you have established is an important and necessary step as you continue to rebuild your practice as you journey to becoming Witch.

To be Witch is to observe not only the magnificent realms of physical nature and learn from these observations, but also to seek out and engage with the Unseen Realms. It is through a thirst for knowledge and deeper understanding that the Witch is bound to establish and nurture a relationship with the forces of the natural world, as well as with entities that exist within the Unseen Realms of existence.

Establishing communication with spirits allows the Witch to receive guidance, insight, and empowerment on her or his journey to becoming Witch, but forming the connection and nurturing the relationships can be challenging. Approaching the Unseen Realms with pure intellectual thought and logic will not successfully align the Witch with spiritual entities. Alignment can only be gained through the integration of the totality of the Witch as a human being, this is clearly illustrated in the first power of The Witches' Pyramid: To Know. The Witch must know, understand, and accept all aspects of her or himself; both the light and pleasant traits, as well as the darker attributes of her or his character. This is not a suggestion or merely an option for consideration, but rather a necessity when seeking to reach out a hand into the ether with the desire for engagement with whomever may be near. Hiding aspects of yourself because they are unattractive or objectionable focuses on the fears you harbor within you and holds no benefit for the Witch, instead hiding these shadows creates a veil of self-deception, which will be fully exploited by spirits with malevolent agendas.

Communication between the Witch and spiritual entities may not always occur through the rite of evocation or invocation and may transpire in other ways such as through: dreams, visions, inspired or automatic writing, divination, omens, serendipity or synchronicity, high frequency ringing in the ears or tingling in the physical body, recurring thoughts or repeated suggestion from different sources, human and nonhuman (animal, bird, fish, reptile, amphibian, and insects) messengers, and wondrous events. It is important to remember that regardless of how communication between the living physical human being and spirit is established, discernment is always necessary for the overall safety of the Witch.

Spiritual entities are similar to human beings in that they are all different and possess a distinctive energetic vibration. This distinction will allow you to better identify the varied spirits with which you will establish contact. As you encounter each entity, you will discover that some emit a denser vibrational energy, while others feel light and airy, and similar to humans, they each will possess a unique personality. There are spirits with a serious or brooding disposition, while others will be playful, but know that each spirit will be motivated by specific desires and not all spirits are seeking to aid the Witch or benefit humanity.

Trusting other Witches and magickal practitioners may be expected within our community, but when communicating with spirits, do not disregard personal discernment, regardless of what you've been told by another Witch about any spiritual entity you encounter. It is in your own best interest to establish the agenda of any spirit you come in contact with and determine for yourself whether you should trust the entity or not. We are a diverse community and each of us holds a unique vibrational energy, which will resonate differently with a spiritual entity even if we are similar to another Witch. None of us are exact replicas of each other nor are we a duplicate of another Witch's vibrational energy and must do our due diligence for our own overall protection and use discernment in our interactions with the Unseen Realms.

My sister Witch, ObsidianFire, may have an established relationship with a spirit known to her as Haniel, and she has come to understand that this spirit is a light being or angel, but when I interact with this same spirit it is my responsibility to discern its intention with me even if I trust ObsidianFire completely. I would be doing a serious disservice to myself if I didn't question the intentions of Haniel. Each of us must be able to distinguish, discriminate, evaluate, and appraise a spirit with our own skills and abilities in order to determine what is truth and what is deception. And even then, this does not assume that a truth determined by one Witch, in my example, ObsidianFire, is a universal truth about that spirit for all who interact with it.

When engaging with spirits, it is paramount for the Witch to maintain control. While misguided spiritual entities cannot physically cause harm, their energetic influence over the Witch and the Witch's environment could produce negative experiences and cause psychic distress. It is for this explicit reason that you should establish and maintain a form of protection such as wards, shields, or a magick Circle when communing with the Unseen Realms. If a relationship with a familiar spirit has been established, the familiar may serve as a ward or act as a mediator for the Witch when she or he is communicating with the Unseen Realms.

Familiar Spirit

The familiar spirit is the most universally known entity connected with the Witch, but within modern Witchcraft it is also the most widely misunderstood. I have encountered many a modern Witch explaining how her cat, Shadow, is her familiar or that his dog, Thor, is his familiar, but I have come to understand that neither is an accurate description of Shadow or Thor. A Witch's familiar is simply not a family pet. In fact, the familiar is not physically incarnated at all, it is incorporeal. It is a spirit, a familiar spirit.

A familiar spirit is a spiritual entity with whom the Witch is closely acquainted. As with other spirits, the familiar possesses free will, a unique personality, and an energetic vibration, which draws the Witch to it and it to the Witch, creating a magickal bond between them that is mutually beneficial; a bond that will grow stronger over time, merging the energies of both into one. A familiar works with the Witch as a mediator, a teacher, a mentor, a magickal partner, a spy, a messenger, a ward, a source of power, and ideally as their bond grows and strengthens, an extension of the Witch her or himself.

The spirit may be housed in a physical vessel, usually an inanimate object, such as a statue, a piece of jewelry, or other ornamental object, though in my personal experience the familiar spirit may also possess a living body, thus appearing to be corporeal, which may have led to the popular misunderstanding that a Witch's familiar is simply her or his family pet.

My familiar spirit has been with me for most (and possibly all) of my life. When I was a young child, I didn't recognize my companion as a familiar spirit. I was unaware of such a term or concept. Instead, I believed that this companion was my friend, one that liked to play Hide-and-Seek with my parents and grandmother, even if they were never interested in playing along. My "imaginary" friend spent hours with me playing in my sandbox and hosting tea parties beneath the old Weeping Willow tree in the backyard. But as I grew older, I accepted the belief that only children had "imaginary" friends. I listened to the adults who told me that I had an overactive imagination and dismissed the idea that my invisible friend was real. I found it difficult to ignore her, especially when she brought others for me to meet. I tried to deny the fascination I had for them, but I was repeatedly enticed to spend hours of my time with them in a place beyond our physical reality.

It wasn't until I began studying Wicca that I came across the concept of a familiar spirit. It was during this time that I owned a black and white tuxedo cat named, Bandit. He was about ten years old at that time. Our relationship had always been special. I found myself relating to him as if he were a person I knew from my past, only disguised as a cat. The idea that he was the "imaginary" friend from my childhood had entered my mind on more than one occasion, but it seemed silly so I never really gave it merit – not until after his death.

Bandit died in early 2007. I had been practicing Wicca for two years and with my limited understanding I knew that Bandit to some degree had been my working partner; a sentry while I worked within cast Circle, a battery for me when I didn't pull enough energy on my own, and my emissary when I desired spiritual counsel. My practice felt less effective when he left, but I blamed the change on my grief.

A few months later I decided I wanted to adopt another cat, and after a few visits to the local animal rescue, a fluffy black kitten came home with us. I named him Alchemy. As he grew older, it became clear to me through his personality and behavior that Bandit had returned to me in another vessel. It was with this revelation that I began seeking a greater understanding of my relationship with Bandit and through meditation and contemplation I gained the understanding I sought. My "imaginary" friend from childhood had never left. She was my familiar spirit. She was the spirit that animated Bandit when he was alive and at that body's death transmigrated into the body of the cat I named Alchemy.

Alchemy died in July of 2018, before we moved

to Seattle, and although I have since adopted a new cat, named Oberon, it is obvious that my familiar spirit no longer possesses a living body.

Beloved Dead

The Beloved Dead are the personal human ancestors of the Witch. They include not only those related by blood, but also those that we viewed as family members through marriage or deep intimate friendship. Each Beloved possesses the same personality and character traits as they did when they were alive in the Physical Realm. If Grandma Isabel was feisty and independent in life, she will be the same in spirit when you interact with her, though she will possess greater insight and understanding of human life. Each Beloved's energetic vibration will feel recognizable to the Witch who works with them and there will be a familiarity to the interactions between Witch and Beloved that cannot be easily dismissed or ignored.

A Witch's relationship with a Beloved is one of the easiest to establish since a bond existed prior to death; whether the connection was one of blood or emotion. The Beloved Dead work with the Witch as teachers, mentors, guides, companions, messengers, and a source of limitless power. Unlike the familiar spirit, the Beloved Dead have no requirement to be housed in a physical vessel since they have a recognizable bond with physicality through their previous incarnation.

The Witch can aid the bond with their Beloved Dead through the practice of shrine tending. Each Beloved the Witch chooses to work with should have a special place or shrine created specifically for them.

The memorial should include at least one photograph of the Beloved, one of their personal items, or their funeral or mourning card. Offerings should be given to them at their shrine and on a regular basis to aid the Beloved in attaining a more cohesive nature.

The attention the Beloved Dead receive through regular engagement with the Witch is energy given freely to them. Just as humans, being physical in nature, require physical food to sustain us, spirits, being energetic in nature, require energy to sustain them, and offerings fulfill this requirement. While the spirit cannot physically consume the food or drink gifted to them, it is the intention that imbues the offerings that the spirit consumes. It is for this reason that offering Beloved food, drinks, and other items that they enjoyed during their life provide the greatest rewards for the Witch. If Grandma Isabel enjoyed smoking Winston cigarettes and chewing Dentyne gum in life, she would enjoy these things offered to her in death. It's also acceptable to offer incense, especially one crafted specifically for the Beloved, flowers, and conscious acts of kindness such as: reading a chapter from a cherished book, singing the Beloved's favorite song, or simply focusing your attention on the memory of their life and your time together.

My work with the Beloved Dead didn't begin in earnest until I had established my practice in other areas and felt comfortable with what I perceived as the less intimidating aspects of Witchcraft. While I would casually accept my Beloved's insight when practicing divination, I didn't consider working with them in any other ways. I was acquainted with The Dead since I was introduced to them as a teenager by my familiar spirit but I wasn't willing to carelessly enlist their assistance with magickal workings until I felt ready. I gradually nurtured my bond with them by setting up and tending an altar dedicated to my relationship with each of them. Since my transition, the Beloved Dead have been a focus of my Witchcraft and a fount of power for my spells and magickal workings, as well as a personal source of wisdom.

The Ancestors

The Ancestors are the spirits with whom the Witch is bonded with through their Witchcraft. They represent the communion of Witches from time immemorial. This community includes every Witch that lived, those who are well-known historical figures, as well as contemporary Witches who are unknown to the vast majority of us, who may have practiced solitarily in the stillness of the night, deep within the wild forest, beneath the expanse of the desert sky, on a secluded beach, or in the garden behind their home. Together this collection of magickal power comprises the spiritual entity known as The Ancestors. It is likely that the collective will not include your own blood relatives who have died, but it is a possibility if you were born from a hereditary line of Witches.

The Ancestors are drawn to the Witch through magick. The communal energy merges with the Witch's own magick, empowering all the Witch does within her or his Craft. The Ancestors work with the Witch as teachers, mentors, guardians, observers, and an unlimited source of power unlike anything else the Witch will experience. As the Witch's own practice grows and strengthens, The Ancestors presence in her or his own Craft exponentially grows and strengthens.

The Ancestors, like the Beloved Dead, don't require housing within a physical vessel since they were once human beings and have sympathetic bonds with physical life. The Witch should honor The Ancestors, recognizing the knowledge attained and passed down through the generations, along with the past sacrifices given so that we, the modern Witches, are able to practice our Craft. This can be done by creating a memorial, which might include representations or symbols of Witchcraft that appeal to the individual Witch. These items might include recognizable statuary, working tools, tapestries, altar cloths, or other items associated with magick and Witchcraft.

Providing offerings to The Ancestors is acceptable, though the nature of the offerings will again differ between Witches and their personal style in practicing their Craft. What is important to remember is that it isn't the items that are offered that is of importance, but it's the intention imbued within that is vital. If the Witch is absently crafting an incense she or he plans to burn for The Ancestors while thinking about what place to order take-out from, the Witch should refrain from offering the incense as it doesn't hold the proper intention.

The Ancestors have held a place of honor in my Witchcraft since the time I began practicing. When holding ritual for myself or others, I would evoke The Ancestors as part of the Circle casting and ensure that on the eve of Samhain they were given reverence during the celebration.

There are a vast number of spiritual entities that the Witch may communicate with and work with: angels (archangels and guardian angels), ascended masters, astral travelers, Beloved Dead, demons, djinns, dragons, dreamers, elementals, fae, familiars, ghosts, god forms, multidimensional beings, psychic leeches and other parasitic entities, spirit guides, The Ancestors, and tulpas (thoughtforms / servitors), but there are also an infinite number of entities I have not mentioned that exist within the Unseen Realms, so it is important to understand that a spiritual entity's perspective may be completely unfamiliar to the Witch communicating with it. Not all spiritual entities incarnated on Earth and so they may not have a human understanding of life as we know it, although they may have a basic knowledge of how we live. Some spiritual entities may exist within a realm or dimension where the concept of time does not exist, and when communing with them, they may appear or seem dead, but that is not the reality; discernment is what is required to determine the truth of the situation.

Many spirits seek a Witch's attention and actively pursue relationships with us in order to become more cohesive in nature and endure because the majority of such relationships are mutually beneficial. The Witch gains insight to topics and situations she or he doesn't possess direction knowledge of while providing energy to the spirit, allowing it to become a more cohesive presence.

While freely giving etherical food to spiritual entities is not in and of itself a bad thing or a poor choice for the Witch to make, the interaction does have the potential for becoming overwhelming or unmanageable. If either Witch or spirit assumes the role of dictator within the relationship, a boundary has been crossed and the connection between the two will become toxic. At that point it would be beneficial to the Witch to end the relationship; allowing it to continue will ultimately end with either partner causing irrevocably harm to the other. Either the Witch will experience some form of mental or emotional breakdown, or spirit possession, or the spirit will experience energetic erosion.

Exercise: Automatic Writing

Automatic writing allows the Witch to act as a scribe for the Unseen Realm. It is the practice of setting aside your conscious mind to allow your unconscious mind to be influenced by spirits providing you with messages. If you have never attempted to communicate with spirits directly, I find that this is one of the easiest ways to do so other than using a Spirit (Ouija) Board.

You should read through the exercise in its entirety before you attempt it so that you know what visualization you will be using.

The tools for this exercise are basic; a few pieces of blank paper, a working pen, a timer, and a quiet place to sit at a table where you will not be disturbed. Alternatively, you may opt to use your computer and therefore will only need to sit in front of the computer at a table or at your desk, but be certain you can do so without being disturbed.

Take your position at the table. Settle yourself until you feel comfortable with your feet firmly on the floor.

Set your timer for five minutes for the first session. You can increase your time with each consecutive session up to fifteen minutes or until you stop writing.

Grasp the pen loosely in your hand, or if you're sitting at the computer, gently place your fingers on the keyboard.

Breathe deeply a few times and vocalize an open-ended question to which you would like to know the answer. You can address the question to an unspecified spirit, one of your Beloved Dead, or The Ancestors. The question can be something completely personal concerning you or something more generic and applicable to all humanity. Some examples are:

- What do I need to know about my health?
- How can I improve my Witchcraft?
- What is stopping me from getting a promotion at work?
- What would most benefit humanity at this current time?
- How can we heal the Earth?

After vocalizing your query, enter your trance state in whatever way you have successfully done with the previous exercises.

While in your altered state of consciousness, visualize yourself taking dictation from a spirit, who is standing behind you while whispering in your ear.

Take time with the visualization, allowing it to develop organically.

Once you are able to hold the visualization in your mind, allow your hand to write whatever you hear in your mind or audibly with your ears. If you are sitting at a keyboard, allow your fingers to type what you hear.

Allow the words to flow from you without thought to what you are writing. Do not pay attention to the words. Don't try to control them. Type everything you hear, reserving any judgement on what you are writing. Don't edit yourself. Don't worry about spelling or syntax or grammar.

Allow this process to continue until your timer goes off or until you've stopped actively writing.

Put down your pen or save your word document and stand up.

Step away from your chair and stretch. Get a glass of water and drink and / or have a snack. Do whatever you usually do to ground yourself.

Once you're grounded, go back and read what you've written. Search the document for phrases, sentences, or words that make sense and hold meaning for you that might answer the question you posed at the beginning of the session.

Don't be discouraged or frustrated as automatic writing, like any other practice within Witchcraft, takes practice; a few sessions per week is bound to yield some sort of results.

Keep the paper(s) tucked in your journal or saved on your computer and record any messages that you can detect or uncover from what you wrote during your session. Remember to record the date, time, and any conditions within your environment or within yourself that may have influenced the session.

Exercise: Evocation

The simplest definition for evocation is the act of summoning a spiritual entity, deity, or other energetic force into your sacred space. This means that the spirit is in your presence, not within your body. If you are a Witch who casts Circle including the act of Calling the Quarters then you have practiced evocation.

I suggest that you read through this entire exercise before attempting it. And before you actually begin, you will need to establish some form of protection for yourself. If you already have an established sacred space then performing this exercise there is ideal. If you are a Witch who casts a Circle with or without Calling Quarters then performing this exercise within that Circle is acceptable.

Consider what spirit, deity, or other energetic force you wish to evoke. I suggest evoking an energy that you already have some knowledge about such as: a deity you've studied, the spirit of your Beloved Dead, a spirit guide, animal ally, guardian angel, or a Nature Spirit. When contemplating which spiritual entity you will evoke, I encourage you to consider the wise words of H. P. Lovecraft in his short story, *The*

Case of Charles Dexter Ward: "Do not call up that which you cannot put down."

After deciding on what or whom you will be evoking in your space, consider what you would like to experience during this time. What is your intention for evoking this spirit, deity, or energetic force? Would you like to establish a relationship with this deity? Do you have questions for the spirit? Are you seeking protection from the spirit guide or guardian angel? Are you looking for insight into the nature of this particular Nature Spirit?

With your intention in mind, it is time to write your evocation. I find that with planning what I will say during the summoning, I am able to perform the evocation more successfully, but if unprompted evocations are more aligned with your practice and you feel that you are inclined to work that way, I encourage you to do so. Just be aware that vocalizing your evocation is important as I discussed in the first chapter.

My written evocations are simple and repetitious in nature. The following is one I've used successfully numerous times in the past when evoking the Egyptian goddess Isis:

> *"Hail Isis - full of wisdom,*
> *Lady of Many Faces,*
> *Mistress of Hidden Magicks,*
> *Blessed are you from whom all becoming arose!*
> *Blessed are you protector of the dead!*
> *Mighty Isis, Mother Goddess!*
> *I summon you. I summon you.*
> *Mighty Isis, Mother Goddess!*
> *I summon you."*

After you've written your evocation and have it committed to memory, it is time to prepare yourself for the summoning. I generally find that if I'm not evoking the elements and the primordial energies of the divine masculine and feminine for a spell casting, I will check the phase of the Moon to determine which energies might work best with the spiritual entities or force I am seeking to evoke, doing my best to align the energies to aid with the success of the experience.

When the time approaches for the evocation, you will want to prepare by performing a cleansing and consecration on yourself.

Following the consecration, enter your sacred space, and proceed with entering a trance state. Here you will visualize the spirit or force that you are evoking. Allow the visualize to form slowly so that you are able to create a strong experience.

Once you are able to hold the visualization firmly in your mind, recite aloud your evocation. Repeat the words until you sense an energetic shift occur within your sacred space, this usually indicates that the spirit or force has joined you.

At this point you are free to engage with the spirit or force to fulfill your desired intention.

After you have fulfilled the intention, it is prudent to release the spiritual entity that you've summoned. Just as you evoked with spoken words, I suggest releasing in a similar way:

"Farewell Isis - full of wisdom,
Lady of Many Faces,
Mistress of Hidden Magicks,
Blessed are you from whom all becoming arose!
Blessed are you protector of the dead!

Mighty Isis, Mother Goddess!
I release you. I release you.
Mighty Isis, Mother Goddess!
I release you."

Repeat the words until you sense an energetic shift occur within your sacred space. You should feel the energy shift back to what it was prior to the evocation. If you sense any excess energy lingering, I suggest transferring it to the Earth. I encourage you to ground yourself before leaving your sacred space.

Remember to record your experience in your journal, noting the date, time, and any other conditions within your environment or within yourself that may have influenced the evocation. Record the name of the spiritual entity you evoked, and / or other details that would allow you to recognize the entity again if you were to meet it in the future, and the results of your experience.

Exercise: Invocation

An invocation is a serious request for a deity or other spiritual entity to possess a physical vessel, usually the body of the individual performing the invocation. This means that when the Witch invokes a spirit, you are sharing your body with a foreign spiritual entity. If you are a Witch who performs a Wiccan type ritual, which includes the act of Drawing Down the Moon, then you have practiced invocation.

Do not attempt this exercise until you have successfully completed the previous exercise, *Exercise: Evocation*. And as with the previous exercise, I suggest that you also read through this one before attempting it.

Before you begin, you will need to establish some form of protection for yourself. If you already have an established sacred space, then performing this exercise there is ideal. If you are a Witch who casts a Circle, then performing this exercise within that Circle is acceptable.

Consider what spirit, deity, or other energetic force you wish to invoke. I suggest invoking an energy that you are familiar with, perhaps a deity you work with or with whom you previously evoked, or one of your spirit guides. When performing an invocation, it is important to possess a strong sense of Self and to trust the entity you are invoking.

After choosing the spiritual entity, consider your intention for the exercise. What type of experience do you desire? Are you looking for insight into the nature of this particular entity? Would you like to gain deeper understanding of this deity?

With your intention in mind, write your invocation. As with the previous exercise, if working in a more spontaneous way is your inclination then I encourage you to do so, but remember that your invocation, whether prewritten or unprompted, should be spoken aloud at the proper time. My invocations are written similarly to my evocations. The following is an example I used to invoke the goddess, Danu:

"Oh Danu, I invoke thee, Great Mother,
By the great Mysteries,
By the mighty powers of the Air, Earth, and Seas,
I invoke thee, Danu. I invoke thee.

As you stand at the portal; to The Elemental Kingdoms,
Allow me to see with your eyes.
Creatrix who birthed all things into being,
Bring forth to me the key to your wisdom and knowledge.
Enlighten me with the secrets of life everlasting.

I destroy my ego.
I release all fear.
I open my heart to your presence.
I feel your presence within me.
Your love within my heart,
Your wisdom within my mind.

Oh Great Mother Danu!
I invoke thee. I invoke thee.
Oh Great Mother Danu,
I invoke thee!"

After you've written your invocation and have it committed to memory, it is time for preparation. Just as with an evocation, if I'm not holding a ritual and invoking a god or goddess, I will check the Moon phases and determine which energies will align with the deity or spirit I am seeking to invoke.

During the twenty-four hours prior to the invocation, it is best to drink plenty of water and to either fast or eat small meals or snacks as this will ensure that your physical body isn't exerting all your energy on the digestion of the food you've consumed. You will want this energy spent on the invocation.

Cleansing and consecration are necessary, just as with evocation, and following the consecration, you will enter your sacred space.

Take your time entering a trance state and visualizing the deity or spiritual entity you are invoking. Allow the visualization to form slowly so that you are able to create a strong experience.

Once you are able to hold the visualization firmly in your mind, recite aloud the invocation. Repeat the words until you sense an energetic shift occur within your body. Just as with evocation, the shifting energy is a sign that the invocation has been successful.

At this point you are free to engage with the deity or spirit to fulfill your desired intention.

After you have fulfilled the intention, it's prudent to release the deity or spirit that you have invoked, and just as you invoked with spoken words, I suggest releasing in a similar way:

"Oh Danu, I release thee, Great Mother,
By the great Mysteries,
By the mighty powers of the Air, Earth, and Seas,
I release thee, Danu. I release thee.

As I stand in my sacred space; a place between the Kingdoms,
I thank you for allowing me to see with your eyes.
I thank you for bringing forth to me the key to your wisdom and knowledge.
I thank you for enlightening me with deeper understanding of the nature of life and humanity.

I release thee, Danu.

Oh Danu, Great Mother,
My heart remains open to your presence.
I hold your love within my heart,
And your wisdom within my mind.
I am forever your daughter and priestess.

Oh Great Mother Danu!
I release you. Farewell."

Repeat the words until you feel the energetic shift occur within your body. If you sense any excess energy lingering, transfer it to the Earth, then ground and center yourself before leaving your sacred space.

I would also encourage you to eat a meal, or at least a snack, which will ground you into physicality. Feeling light headed or disconnected is common after a successful invocation, so continue the practice of grounding.

Remember to record your experience in your journal; noting the date, time, and any other conditions within your environment or within yourself that may have influenced the invocation. Record the name of the deity or spiritual entity you invoked, and / or other details that would allow you to recognize the entity again if you were to meet it in the future, and the results of the experience you had.

Chapter 7

The Elementals and Elements

Reflecting on the personal relationship you have with the energies of the natural world is something that the Witch does on a fairly regular basis, but as you work to reconstruct your practice within Witchcraft, this contemplation becomes a vital step in getting *"back to the basics"*. The journey to becoming Witch begins with cultivating a relationship with Mother Nature.

The Elementals, sometimes referred to as nature spirits, are living etherical energy that vibrate at a higher energetic frequency than any physical form found on the planet and therefore align with the unseen Elemental Realm. They are vital energies that are not only required for existence on the planet, but they, in their very essence, are the building blocks of life itself and influence all aspects of life living on the Earth.

They are the consciousness of the elements and in a singular formation, and when manifested in physical matter, are expressed as their corresponding element of either Air, Fire, Earth, or Water. They are the natural forces that exist within each element, aligning them closely with, but separate from, the vibration of the Physical Realm. All natural forms found on the planet: trees, plants, flora, mountains, lakes, ponds, moss, and fungi, hold the presence of The Elementals.

It would benefit the Witch to deliberately work with The Elementals within her or his Craft through the practice of evocation or summoning, as attempting to invoke or command The Elementals will only lead to great distress and failure. This is due to the fact that The Elementals are feral and untamed in their natural state of being, so it is best to come to understand and befriend them, not to directly invoke them nor seek control of them. The Witch who lives in harmony with her or himself and the planet will find it easy to befriend The Elementals, and once your respect is gained and a relationship is established, they will aid you with your spell casting and magickal workings, as your intentions will most likely align with theirs, granting you a connection and access to the full power that nature possesses.

Without an established relationship, The Elementals are still responsible for the physical manifestation of the Witch's thoughtforms, allowing that which is etherical in its nature to become matter. They translate the Witch's intention that has formed in the Astral Realm through the Elemental Realm and manifest it into the Physical Realm. The benefit in establishing a relationship with The Elementals is that this process is done quicker and without resistance.

To work with The Elementals, the Witch must go to them and not wait for them to present themselves to you. You must align your energetic vibration with theirs as they are unable to move beyond the Unseen

Realms. This task can be accomplished by the use of clairvoyance, casting a magick Circle, practicing astral travel, or entering a trance while in sacred space. It is then that the Witch may perceive and interact with the embodied Elementals in the forms of sylphs, salamanders, gnomes, and undines.

The physical manifestation of The Elementals: Air, Fire, Earth, and Water, are the energetic substance of all creation. Everything that you can see, hear, smell, taste, and touch is manifested in the physical form of matter, which is made up of all or a combination of these elements. Understanding the interconnectedness between the elements, the natural world, and sentient beings, is important for the Witch as it clearly defines the relationship between all seen and unseen things in existence. Establishing and nurturing a personal relationship with The Elementals is a natural expression of this interconnectedness as the human body is a direct manifestation of the elements within a singular form; Air is breath, Fire is Will, Earth is body (flesh, bones, and organs), and Water is blood.

Each element can be viewed as either being dynamic and projective in their nature, or receptive and accepting. This concept is important when using energy to manifest the intention of the Witch in the Physical Realm through magick and should be considered when seeking correspondences for a spell or magickal working. It is commonly acknowledged and accepted that the elements of Air and Fire are projective and these energies are sent outward to cause change or transformation, while the elements of Earth and Water are receptive, which allows the change or transformation to occur within.

Although the elements align with the behavior of

being projective or receptive, each also holds a specific energy that will manifest itself to the Witch in an entirely unique and personal way, even if it may appear at first glance to be completely unconventional or lacking of any traditional correspondence that the Witch may expect when considering that particular element. For example, within my Witchcraft the element of Earth doesn't tend to appear to me as trees, or plants, or mountains, or stones, instead when I work with the element of Earth, I interact with Kodama, the nature spirits within Japanese folklore. I am not of Japanese descent and generally only have a slight interest in Japanese culture, but I do recognize that where I live there is a great Asian influence and it certainly affects the land on which I reside. I assume this is where that energy has collected, within the soil beneath my feet, within the land on which the house I live in was built. When I call upon the element of Earth within my Craft, this is the energy that responds to me, the whispers that sing to me. Perhaps it is the appearance that The Elemental of Earth has taken for me instead of the gnome I might expect, but regardless of the appearance, I know it is the energy of Earth and, as such, I allow myself to be open to its power.

Relating to the local environment, both the natural world and the manmade structures within the city or town in which you live, is paramount for your Craft. Acclimating yourself to the energy and the shifts that will occur within the community and your home will enable you to be more successful with your spell casting and magickal workings since the energy is interconnected. Attempting to cast a spell with the intention of growth and prosperity when everyone in the home is dealing with some type of introspection or Shadow Work will be counterproductive and require a lot of effort and Will for it to manifest. Instead it would be more effective to work with the energies that are already present and cast a spell to clear obstacles or gain insight.

Spending time within the landscape, paying attention to the weather, to the light and climate of the day and season, will allow you to adjust correspondences when necessary or to completely readjust a working that you are planning and crafting. Connecting with the nature spirits of the local plants, trees, flowers, and fungi will be of a great benefit to you, as will connecting with the local species of animals, insects, and birds. Locating and visiting local places of power such as landmarks, graveyards, cemeteries, and any energy vortexes will aid in your alignment with the local energy stream and provide you the opportunity to connect, if you so wish, with any spirits that you meet in those places.

From my own experience, it was easier for me to make contact with The Elementals in Washington state than it was in Massachusetts. While new apartment buildings and other structures are being constructed regularly, the natural surroundings remain prevalent in my neighborhood. The property we are renting sits on a small plot of land that was most neglected before we moved in. It truly appeared abandoned, due to the work schedule and social obligations of the owner. Once I was settled inside our new home, I was able to spend time acclimating with the energy of the land. I began by introducing myself to the nature spirits, by spending time doing general landscaping, gardening, and setting up bird feeding stations in our yard. This provided me numerous opportunities to spend quality time to speak directly to The Elementals while working side by side with them.

Exercise: Aligning with the Elements

This exercise was designed for the Witch to experience a personal alignment with the energy of each of the elements: Air, Fire, Earth, and Water, so that she or he is able to determine the difference between them and be better able to evoke the energy of each element into her or his sacred space or Circle.

It is best if each element is worked with for approximately one lunar cycle, though you may extend or shorten the time spent with each element if you find that the one lunar cycle isn't an appropriate length of time for your practice.

As you consider the energy of each element you will do the following in the order presented here:

- Journal
- Observe
- Experience
- Contemplate

Journal: Write the name of the element you are aligning with during the lunar cycle on the top of an empty page in your journal. Below the title, write all the words you associate with this element. Allow your mind the freedom to explore the concept of the element. Don't second guess any word you write and don't cross out any of the words. As you work with the energy of the element during this time, you should add to the list as you uncover any new associations you make.

Observe: Find ways in which you are able to witness the interaction between the physical world and the energies of the element that you are aligning with during this time. In your journal, record all your observations and feelings about the experiences you witness.

The following are ideas on how you could observe the elements energy. You're not required to use any of them, they're simply provided as examples of what you might do to witness the manifestation.

Air: Bird watch, watch the clouds go by, lay beneath a tree and watch leaves as they move in the breeze, observe the smoke from burning incense, star gaze.

Fire: Watch something burning, study a candle flame, witness the sunrise and / or sunset.

Earth: Watch squirrels (or other land mammals) play, study the movement of trees.

Water: Watch a fountain, study the movement of a waterfall or river, observe water going down the drain, watch fish swim in an aquarium.

Experience: Take the initiative to explore the influence of the element for yourself as many times during the lunar cycle as possible. Fully immerse yourself in the energy of the element so that you're able to use as many of your senses (sight, sound, smell, taste, feel) as possible during the experience. Remember to record the interactions, which should include your feelings and any other sensations that occurred for you during this time.

As with the above suggestions for observation, you are not required to use any of the following ideas to experience the energy of each element, again they are just ideas to get you started:

Air: Fly a kite, use a pinwheel, stand in front of an electric fan, blow bubbles, play on a swing, go outside during a strong wind, blow the dried seeds of a dandelion, take a ride in a helicopter, hot air balloon, or Ferris wheel.

Fire: Cook food over a flame, burn some wood in a campfire or fireplace, light a candle, sit outside in the sunshine.

Earth: Plant a tree or garden, pick apples, walk barefoot, mow the lawn, trim a bush or cut wood, rake leaves, build a sandcastle, gather rocks, take a hike, go camping, sit with your back against a tree, lay on the ground.

Water: Swim in a pond or pool, wade in the ocean, walk in the rain, take a bath, play in puddles, wash your car, water the garden, go snorkeling, build a snowman, have a snowball or water balloon fight, gather seashells.

Contemplate: Consider how you're best able to incorporate the energy of the element into your Witchcraft and record the ideas you formulate in your journal.

Chapter 8

Sacred Space

It is during unstable spans of transition or the sluggish time of personal stagnation, whether of the mundane or magickal variety, that our sacred space is often neglected, left to gather dust while the magick we built within is left to dissipate. Our sacred space is a physical cornerstone on which we build the structure of our practice, so it is one of the key elements the Witch must consider when getting *"back to the basics"*.

Sacred space is an area set aside for communion with the gods, The Ancestors, Beloved Dead, and other spirits that the Witch recognizes and acknowledges. It is a place to cast spells, do magickal workings; simply, a safe place in which to practice Witchcraft. For some Witches, sacred space is their cast Circle, but depending on the way the Witch practices their magick, this may not be so.

All religions and spiritual paths recognize the importance of sacred space. These locations are where churches, temples, and shrines were erected and where cemeteries and graveyards are situated. The place where divine contact occurred, the birth place of a recognized spiritual teacher, the village where a great master lived, or where mass deaths occurred, are also recognized by many people to be sacred spaces.

For the Witch, sacred space is most commonly a personal place established by the practitioner in her or his home or on their property, which holds their accumulated personal energy and magick. Each time a Circle is cast or a magickal working is done in the space the residual energies raised by the Witch are returned to the ground (or floor) where the magick was performed. After time this accumulated energy will create a vortex of power that can be harnessed the next time an act of magick is performed there.

If the sacred space is established outside, within the natural environment, and the Witch established a relationship with The Elementals, they may imbue the space with their own energies, thus adding to the power that has accumulated there; the same can be said of any other spiritual entity that may reside in the environment. If the sacred space is established within the home, the energies of the other individuals that reside in the home and any spirits that linger may add to the power, unless the Witch takes care to suspend them outside the allocate sacred space.

Not all Witches cast a Circle, but within some traditions of Witchcraft, spell castings and magickal workings are done within one and this Circle is considered sacred space. The purpose of a Circle is to define a specific area that is separated from the laws of the Physical Realm, a space beyond the bounds of time, beyond birth and death, where all energies converge, where anything is possible and the Witch's abilities are limitless.

The Circle is often delineated by candles, ribbon, salt, sand, or other natural substance, and is sometimes inscribed with sacred words, names, or symbols after it has been cast by the Witch with the ritual blade or wand. The Witch's altar usually holds a prominent place within the Circle either at the center or at one of the cardinal points, commonly the North or East, and will act as the anchor for the raised energy.

Whether the Witch casts a Circle, or whether magick is performed in a different type of sacred space, the only concepts, rules, and laws that are defined are those that the Witch believes to be true. It is those beliefs that are applied to the spell casting or magickal working. There are no limits to magick, just as there are no boundaries to energy. Everything is possible and the only morality in question is that which is held by the Witch. This is the precise reason as to why the Witch is required To Know themselves. If you do not know what you believe and why you believe what you believe, you could be unconsciously sabotaging the magick you do in your sacred space; you could be limiting your own magick. There are no absolutes because everything is shifting and changing including you, the Witch. You are not the same Witch today as you were last year, or last month, or last week, or even yesterday. You are always on a journey of becoming, which means that today you may judge a spell as malevolent and believe it is unacceptable, but when you consider that same spell next week or next year, you may perceive it as benevolent. Witchcraft is always subjective.

I have had experiences within a cast Circle, as well as within sacred space, that I would label incredible, and I am convinced that they would not have happened within mundane reality because of the vastly opposing beliefs held by the general population and the limitations that society recognizes within our shared reality. This is the prime reason that I create and maintain sacred space within my home. When I cast a spell or do a magickal working it is imperative that I suspend all unaligned and dissonant energy outside of my space so that my magick will manifest in the quickest time possible. I recognize the power I hold as Witch even if the general population doesn't and I refuse to allow them to negate that power within my Craft.

Maintaining sacred space requires dedication and diligence, but the results of your efforts are worthwhile and will be proven through the continued success of the castings and workings done within its boundaries. Incorporating the task of maintaining your sacred space can be simple and easily included in your daily devotions or ritual, much akin to the routine of getting ready for work or school each morning. For example, once a month, during the full Moon, cleanse the space again, or reimbue the crystal grid you originally constructed, or feed the wards that guard your space, which is what I do each month to maintain the sanctity of my sacred space.

Consistently casting Circle in the same spot in your home or outdoors will create a sacred space, just as practicing your Craft within that space will aid in maintaining its sanctity without any extra effort on your part. Allowing dust to gather on your altar or neglecting to spend time in your sacred space will allow the energy to become stagnant and eventually erode and dissipate; returning your sacred space back into simply space.

Exercise: Establishing Sacred Space

If you work within a magick Circle for every magickal act you perform, then establishing your sacred space may simply be the act of casting your Circle. For this exercise, I encourage you to outline your usual Circle casting within your journal, but take time to contemplate the motives for casting the Circle, as well as the reasons you perform the acts you do when you cast. For example, if you walk clockwise when casting Circle, explain the purpose in doing so. Why it is necessary for your casting? If you call Quarters, explain why you include this practice in your casting. What is the purpose of the evocation? How would the casting be incomplete without evoking the Quarters?

If you are a Witch who does not work within a cast Circle, then for this exercise take time to establish your sacred space. Your first step is to consider the location. Take time to walk around your home, both inside and outdoors, to find the perfect spot that will work for you. The location you choose should allow you to feel comfortable and be uninterrupted while you work your Craft. It is appropriate to have both an indoor location and a space outside as well. If you will be spending an equal amount of time in both locations, you may want to establish both areas as sacred spaces.

Once you have identified the location, it is time to cleanse the space. Physically sweep and mop the floor or vacuum and shampoo the carpet if necessary. Dust the walls, wash the curtains and windows, and ensure that the space is physically clean. If your location is outside, rake and mow the lawn, pick up litter that may have accumulated in the area, and ensure that the space is clear of obstacles you may trip over, so that when you work your Craft will be unhindered by debris.

Open the windows of your indoor space, if there are any, to allow the air to circulate. If there are no windows, or your space is outside, then move about the area, stirring any stagnant energy that might have collected there over time. Sweep, ring bells, beat drums, sing or play music, clap your hands and dance in your chosen spot. Fill the area with your energies, claiming it as your sacred space.

Once you have stirred the energy, the next step is for you to spend time aligning with the combined vibrations and connect with the energy of the space. Relax in your chosen space. Practice meditation there using whatever style that allows you to enter a trance state, granting you the ability to explore the energy of your chosen space. Consider if this energy aligns well with your own. Do you feel welcomed?

At this point, if you are comfortable with the place you've chosen as your sacred space, it's time to consecrate the area as you would any other magickal tool. During your consecration rite, I encourage the Witch to vocalize some form of the following statement: "This space is consecrated and empowered by my hand and by my Will. So mote it be." This area has now been transformed into your sacred space.

Within your space, position any furniture and tools you will require for your practice, while ensuring that you have room to move during your castings and workings. Don't forget to include any light sources that you may need while working in the dark or at night. If this is an outdoor location, you may be unable to keep the furniture and items within your sacred space due to the weather, so be certain you have a way to easily move your items from an inside storage area to this outdoor location.

Once all the items are positioned within your sacred space, set protection along the boundary. If the area is within your home or outside, protection is necessary to safeguard your space from foreign energies that may not be aligned with the intended purpose of your space. Wards, familiars, and servitors are ideal for maintaining protection, just be sure to feed them regularly.

And finally, decorate your sacred space with appropriate items that aid in building the energetic momentum of your intention for this sacred space.

The last step to this process of establishing your sacred space is to record the date and time you began and completed the process in your journal. Don't forget to include the location and a brief description of your space, along with a sketch and your thoughts and insights about the area. I urge you to include thoughts about your experience establishing the spot as sacred. The following are questions to consider:

- What motivated you to choose this location?

- What significance do the particular items you chose to decorate the space have?
- What did the energy feel like before you established the space?
- What did the energy feel like after you finished the process?
- Did you feel a shift in energies occur? If so, what did that feel like?
- How did it feel to integrate your own energies with that of the location you chose?
- Was the merging a difficult process or did the energies meld easily? Why do you think this was?

Chapter 9

Magickal Tools

Most religions and spiritual practices possess certain objects that are used specifically for ritual purposes, but the items are not necessary to the practice and hold no power save for that which is imbued by the practitioner. This idea is also true within the practice of Witchcraft. It is because magickal tools symbolize complex energies that they aid the Witch with the manifestation of intention by enriching the ritual held, magickal working done, or spell that is cast. When the Witch chooses to use a magickal tool, she or he is not only aligning with the energies held by that specific tool, but also the energies of The Ancestors and all other Witches, present and future, that will use the same tool in their Craft. Think about that for a moment and consider the vast well of power that is available to you through magickal tools.

As we continue to get "*back to the basics*", we will reacquaint ourselves with some of the more common tools used by the Witch and the reasons for using them within your own Craft.

Because our magickal tools are used during acts of magick, it is important that they are aligned with our personal vibration and are not tainted by other people's energy. This means that it is vital that we cleanse and consecrate each tool prior to working magick with them.

Cleansing, which can be done in a variety of ways, energetically washes the item of any impurities or residual energies that it may have collected since it was consecrated, but a cleansing will not desecrate the item, and the energies of the consecration will remain imbued in the tool. If a Witch desires to remove the imbued energies from a consecration, then a purification must be performed.

Purifying an item will return the energies of the tool to its natural energetic state thus removing all other energies, whether the energy was intentionally imbued from a consecration rite or is simply residual energies from other outside sources. Purification will remove most energies, but not all energies.

Spiritual entities possess a strong vibrational frequency and will and are likely to remain energetically bound to an item even after a purification rite is done. It will be necessary to perform an exorcism to banish the spiritual entity from the item or vessel, thus severing the energetic connection that was previously established during the possession.

Consecration is a rite done by a Witch to denote that an item or tool is sacred and to dedicate it for a specific purpose, both in the Physical Realm and Astral Realms. Consecration is usually done only once to an item after a cleansing, purification, or exorcism. The rite often includes the act of anointing the tool with an oil that has been crafted by the Witch for this sole purpose. Each Witch will perform a consecration rite differently, and I encourage you to find the way that works best within your own Craft.

The Altar

The basic purpose of the earliest altars was to request the presence of the gods. They were often constructed of stone and carved or painted with symbols of animals and deities. In contrast, a Witch's altar today doesn't necessarily hold the same purpose as not all Witches work with the gods. The size and shape of the altar will be determined by how the surface is used within a Witch's Craft. It may be made of any available material, although natural materials are often preferred; wood being a favorite of mine.

Some Witches have small portable altars that they take with them to various locations and that they are able to store or hide away when not in use, while others will have large permanent altars with various items laid out for display, candles often found burning, and with daily offerings being made to their spirits. Regardless of the size and permanency of the altar, it is the work space for spell castings and magickal workings, though it may not be the only place these acts occur. If the Witch casts a Circle, the altar usually holds a prominent place within it either at the center or at one of the cardinal points, commonly the North or East, and will act as the anchor for the energy raised within.

My primary altar has changed twice since I established it. My first was a short curio cabinet that I purchased from a department store. It was on clearance because it had been the display model.

There was slight damage on the legs, but otherwise it was the perfect size. That altar was with me as an altar (though not my primary one) for twelve years and only left my possession because of the move across country.

My second altar still retains its consecrated purpose and is the one I currently use. It is a wooden dresser that was painted black with gold trim by a previous owner. I purchased it from our former landlady the day we moved into the house we were renting from her in Massachusetts. It was the perfect size and offered plenty of storage with its six drawers. I couldn't part with it when we relocated, so it traveled with us to Washington state.

The Pentacle

The pentacle, a pentagram or five-pointed star encompassed by a circle, commonly sits on the Witch's altar in the center. Within Witchcraft, the pentagram is associated with physical reality and is perceived as a sacred symbol just as it has been by most ancient cultures for many years. You may be surprised to find that the image of both the pentagram and pentacle can still be found on and within most churches, temples, and shrines.

Drawn with the top point up, the pentagram generally represents mind over matter, with that point symbolizing the Witch and the other four points representing the elements of Earth, Air, Fire, and Water, which are present within all human beings. The pentagram in this position also symbolizes the macrocosm of humanity, as a human being standing with arms and legs outstretched, as illustrated beautifully by Leonardo da Vinci's drawing of *The*

Vitruvian Man, circa 1490, resembles a pentagram.

A pentagram set within a circle brings all the elements into unity, the completeness and unification of all that is. The placement of the elements at each point differs depending on the magickal tradition being practiced by the Witch, however traditionally there is recognized a hierarchy among them ranging from the most etherical to the most material and it is this hierarchy that usually determines the placement of the elements at the points of the star.

Within the Craft the main function of the pentacle is to shield and protect, but it also grounds all the energies that are raised and evoked in sacred space. It is associated with the element of Earth, and because of its receptive nature, is recognized as predominately feminine energy. During a consecration rite, the item that is being consecrated is commonly set upon the altar directly on the pentacle.

My large silver pentacle was one of the first tools I purchased from a shop that catered to Witches and other magickal practitioners. I spotted it on the shelf and knew it belonged to me. It's the exact pentacle I used during my first attempt at ritual and is the same one I use today for my spell castings and magickal workings.

The Blade

The blade is our strongest link to The Ancestors, the community of long-deceased Witches. It is a weapon forged in the flames and heat of the element of Fire, and though in today's society we don't use it in battle with, or to defend ourselves against other human beings, we do use it to invoke, command, and banish energies from the Unseen Realms. It is our defense against spirits and unseen entities, making it the most personal of magickal tools, and in being such, it should not be touched by another Witch once it is consecrated. The bond between Witch and blade, established at consecration, will grow stronger with each use.

A double-edged blade of iron or steel, which symbolizes the polarity of the universe, is ideal for the Witch to own. The color and material of the hilt should be associated with the ability to absorb and store energy, which may be called up on by the Witch, if so desired, at a later time for another spell casting, magickal working, or ritual, which makes it the most beneficial tool for casting Circle.

There is a common belief within some traditions that the Witch's blade should never be used for physical purposes, and if doing so, the action will desecrate the blade, but I disagree. I believe that the concern of whether or not the blade has been desecrated originates with the intention of the physical action done with the blade, not whether the Witch was using the blade in a physical or spiritual manner. The Witch should consider her or his motive for choosing to use their blade, asking themselves questions such as: If I use my blade to physically cut this twine, is it part of my spell casting? Does it fulfill a magickal intention, or am I just being lazy by not fetching a pair of scissors to open this package? All consecrated tools, not only the blade, should be used in alignment with their intended purpose.

Being forged in Fire and being projective in its nature, the blade is commonly associated with predominately masculine energies.

Honestly, the blade is my favorite magickal tool, though it is not the first tool I obtained during my journey to becoming Witch. My first blade was an Egyptian athame that I purchased from a new age store at a local mall. It was beautiful with a hilt crafted in the form of a goddess with crossed arms, a winged scarab blade guard, and an unsharpened kris style blade. The sheath was decorated with various hieroglyphs. I worked with that blade for years and only parted with it when the gods of my Craft shifted from the Egyptian pantheon to the Celtic gods.

The blade I use now I obtained from a Witch who was relinquishing her magickal tools. It has no distinctive link to any particular pantheon of gods, but is adorned with a triple crescent moon symbol above its hilt. It has a black handle and double-edged sharpened blade, and though it is simple compared to my first blade, it is the one I favor.

The Wand

Although in some communities the blade and wand are used interchangeably, they hold very different energetic vibrations. The wand is not forged in the heat of fire, but is instead carved from the limbs of a once living tree, and in this way associated with life, not death. It is not typically perceived as a weapon, but as an extension of the Witch's arm, and is used to evoke, invite, and direct energies already present within a sacred space or magickal Circle. As with the blade, a bond between Witch and wand is established at consecration and will grow stronger as the Witch uses it within her or his Craft.

Traditionally the wand is made of wood and is associated with the energy of the tree from which it was carved. It may be as simple as an unadorned stick of oak found in your backyard bark still intact or an elaborately decorated piece of willow carved with magickal symbols and sigils. The length of the wand should be the distance between the Witch's elbow and fingertip.

There are two contradicting thoughts regarding harvesting the wood for a Witch's wand. The first is that the branch should only be taken from the fallen limbs found on the ground, because in this way the tree is left uncut and therefore unharmed, while the other belief is that only branches still attached to the tree should be considered, as these limbs still hold the energy of life desired to be present within a Witch's wand. It is my belief that there are both advantages and disadvantages to both options, but ultimately the Witch should consider their own feelings and beliefs when choosing the origin of their wand. I have owned two different wands that I used within my own Craft over the years: a simple piece of driftwood and a wand made of polished ebony.

While some Witches may opt to use their wand for Circle casting, the blade is the better option since it is aligned with defense and protection against the forces of the Unseen Realms, while the wand is aligned with inviting and directing already present energies and spiritual entities.

Being that the wand is phallic in shape, it is associated with masculine energy, and being it is crafted from a tree branch, the wand is associated with the Air that once passed through the branches.

The Cauldron

For centuries the cauldron was a common sight in every household and would have been used consistently throughout the day for meal cooking. In modern times, however, the cauldron has fallen out of use as cooking vessels, being replaced by modern pans, pots, and rice cookers, but it maintains a common association with Witches. The likely source for the lingering association is the idea that Witches have been around for as long as the cauldron.

Usually made of cast iron, so that it is able to withstand the heat from a fire, whether burning within it or beneath it, the cauldron is a symbol of endurance and is used within Witchcraft for a variety of purposes such as: burning loose incense or petitions, crafting black salt, mixing herbs, spell casting, and scrying.

While some Witches use other bowls, cups, and goblets made of a variety of other materials such as clay, glass, or ceramic, to represent the cauldron, I am of the belief that it is best to own an actual cast iron cauldron or other small iron pot. Possessing and utilizing this tool ensures that the energetic bond between The Ancestors and myself remains strong and powerful. If for some reason you are unable to attain an iron cauldron, in my opinion the next best option is a bowl that resembles a cauldron, something made of ceramic that might be purchased during the Halloween season and would allow you to use it in many of the ways you would use an actual cauldron.

Since cauldrons are round and are shaped like a womb, it corresponds with feminine energy, and since it is made of iron, the most common element found on the planet, forming much of the outer and inner core, it is associated with the element of Earth.

The Broom

The broom is another tool that is often associated

with Witches. The image commonly seen during the Halloween season, or some variation of it, is the old hag wearing a pointed hat, riding her broom past a full Moon. The origin of such an association is that, like the cauldron, it was a standard household item with a practical use, a use which endures even in our modern times. You can find individuals today who are not Witch, and never will identify as Witch, who own a broom and use it in the same manner as it was used years ago, to sweep the floor clear of physical debris.

The Witch utilizes the broom not only in a magickal way, but mundanely as well. It is used when establishing a sacred space, to physically clean the area, while simultaneously stirring any stagnant energy that might have collected there over time. It can be used prior to casting Circle with that same intention, and once the Circle is cast, it can be used to protect and guard it. In this same manner, the broom can be hung by the entrance to your home for protection.

Your broom may also be used as a substitute for your wand, but if you do decide to take advantage of this substitution, it would be wise to consider the type of wood your broom is constructed from, as the energies carried within it may differ from the energies of your wand, and may not correspond with the intention of your planned magickal working or spell casting.

The broom is often associated with the union of masculine and feminine energy due to the phallic appearance of the handle or shaft and the feminine arrangement of the bristles or bushel, which is the symbolism behind the jumping over a broom during wedding ceremonies.

I hang the broom that my husband and I jumped over during our handfasting ceremony on the back of the front door to our home. I don't use that particular broom for physical sweeping because its job is to protect the family while maintaining joy and tranquility within our home. I purchased a broom from a mill store that was made with all-natural materials to do the mundane cleaning of the home, but only after imbuing it with intent.

The Skull

The purpose for working with a skull is to energetically connect with the Unseen Realm of spirits, particularly the deceased human beings with whom you are magickly bound to: your Beloved Dead and The Ancestors. After evoking these spirits into your sacred space, the skull provides them with a vessel in which to occupy for the duration of the spell casting, magickal working, or rite.

It might seem ideal for the Witch to possess an authentic human skull for your altar, and while purchasing a human skull is perfectly legal in the United States, it might not be the best option for you nor the most economical one. The vibrational energy of the person whose skull you end up purchasing may be in direct conflict with your own energy, and just as we don't get along with every human being we meet in the Physical Realm, it would be foolish of us to believe that we will get along with every spirit we encounter. The owner of the skull that you bought, now sitting prominently on your altar in your sacred space, could leave you with a situation that requires your immediate attention. And then there's the consideration of the price of an ethically obtained human skull. They are rather expensive. For example, at the time of this writing, I was able to locate online a normal male human skull imported from India from *The Bone Room* for around two thousand American dollars.

While it may not be desirable, it is practical to own a replica of a human skull made from resin or other material. Keep in mind that if you choose to purchase a replica made from crystal or wood, it would be beneficial to consider the energies that the material already holds, as either may already possess a spiritual entity that would lead you to the same issues as possessing an authentic human skull.

The two skulls that I personally work with in my Craft are made of resin and are approximately five inches tall. They work as successfully as an authentic human skull would for the purpose intended.

The Skeleton Key

Keys have been in existence for thousands of years. We are all familiar with the unique pieces of jagged metal and their purpose. Each of us have possessed a key or two over the course of our lifetime, perhaps keeping them neatly together on a key ring so as not to lose them, because we knew that the only way to access what was being safeguarded by the lock was the matching key. If we lost the key, it would be difficult to gain access to what was within or beyond.

House keys, apartment keys, car keys, office keys, keys that opened a safety deposit box at the bank, a file cabinet at work, the padlock on your storage unit or backyard shed, the old trunk you took with you to college, the locker at the gym, Grandma's suitcase in the attic, or your old red diary; we've all owned and used metal keys even if they are nearly obsolete in today's society, because as with all things, even the key has evolved over time. Today it's unlikely that a guest checking in at a hotel will be given a metal key, instead they will be handed a keycard, which will electronically open the door to their room for the duration of their stay. While the keycard may be easier to manage, it's not as visceral as the metal key.

Skelton keys are used within the Craft as programable items that will allow the Witch to easily access various locations within the mindscape such as: a working chamber in the Astral Realm, or the ethereal temple erected to Lilith that the Coven created during a group meditation, or a meeting place you mentally constructed for the time you commune with Great-Aunt Clara.

Each programmed key is used as a shortcut when traveling to these Unseen Realms, as they will quickly unlock the specific vibrational frequency, allowing the Witch to align with the desired "place". It will also secure the energetic frequency, protecting it from foreign energy and unwanted entities. The keys allow passage into the places that exist behind locked barriers, to liminal spaces, and the mind. They're not only for gaining access, but also setting boundaries.

You can find skeleton keys in a variety of places, from eBay to flea markets and thrift shops, and pay anywhere from one dollar to five dollars per key. I found the keys I resonate with the best and that work easily for me were the ones that I purchased at yard sales and local fairs.

These are the more common tools that I use within my Craft, but they are not the only tools available to the Witch. I would not be surprised to know that you own a tool that I have neglected to mention in this chapter and find that it is vital to your Witchcraft. Since our practices are personal, it is not unusual to possess tools that are special to us and may not make sense to any other Witch. As you reestablish your Craft, the most important point for you to consider is understanding your particular reason and motivation for using any specific tool, whether it is one of the common tools I've discussed here, or whether it is one of a more personal nature.

Exercise: Crafting Anointing Oil

Once crafted this oil can be used in all your consecration rites. If you already have an oil that you use and find that it works successfully, then there is no need for you to craft this one. I am providing you with my own recipe in case you're seeking a change.

For this exercise you will need:

- two glass jars with secure lids (peanut butter jars are an ideal size)

- one small glass bottle with secure topper
- a sieve or coffee filter
- a carrier oil (grapeseed, sweet almond, or olive)
- fresh herbs that are associated with protection, purification, and psychic abilities (Cedar, Cinnamon, Lilac, Mint, Marjoram, Patchouli, Rosemary, and / or Thyme)

You needn't use all of these herbs I listed as they are simply suggestions. I encourage you to research the associations and correspondences of the herbs you choose for this oil.

Wash and dry the two jars, bottle, and fresh herbs thoroughly. It is vital that no moisture is introduced into the oil as it will become prone to bacteria growth and turn rancid.

Once your herbs are completely dried, bruise them by gently pounding them with a pestle or mallet; this will release their natural oils and aroma.

Next, place the bruised herbs in one of the two glass jars and add the oil until the herbs are completely submerged. Close the jar with its corresponding lid and place in a sunny spot. Be sure to shake the jar daily.

After a week, drain off the oil into the other clean dry jar using a sieve for larger herbs or coffee filter for smaller ones. Smell the oil. If you find that the aroma is not strong enough, add more of the same herbs to the new jar and secure the lid. Place the jar back in the sun for another week, shaking it daily.

Wash and dry the used glass jar thoroughly.

After another week, drain off the oil into the first jar using a sieve or coffee filter and smell the oil again. If you are pleased by the smell, pour the oil into the clean, dry, glass bottle and use it in your consecration rituals.

Be sure to record your recipes within your journal so that you are able to recraft the anointing oil when you need more of it.

Exercise: Setting the Altar

The first step in setting up your altar is to consider its desired location. Is this altar going to hold a permanent spot within your sacred space, or will it be moved from indoors to an outside location when you cast Circle? Or are you in need of an altar that can be stored in a closet when not in use? If it is going to be kept in a permanent position within your sacred space, consider why you are choosing that particular spot. What is the motivation for selecting that place? The answer to where it will be located will aid you in considering the size and transportability of your altar. Just as with sacred space, it is appropriate to have more than one altar; a permanent altar and a temporary one that you bring with you to numerous locations.

Once you have identified your altar's location, it is time to seek it out. While in your sacred space, use your skills as Witch to visualize your altar. Take time to experience yourself at your altar. Run your hands over its surface. What material is it made from? Is it a new piece or is it an antique? Look at it from all perspectives. Was it crafted specifically for you or did you find it in a shop or online and purchase it for yourself? How large is it? Can you stand before it or do you sit in front of it? Does it have a scent? Does it have drawers or other storage space? If it has doors or drawers, do they make noise when you open them?

Journal your visualization experience, including the answers to the questions above and any other insights you had pertaining to your altar.

When your altar has manifested for you, and when you have it in your possession, it's time to cleanse it.

Physically clean the altar; inside and out. I frequently use Florida Water for this purpose, but have also brewed my own wash using a mixture of distilled water and herbs.

After cleansing it, it's time to consecrate the altar as you would any other magickal tool. Just as I suggest vocalizing a declaration of consecration for your sacred space, I encourage the same for your altar in whatever wording you prefer. Don't forget to anoint the altar with your newly crafted anointing oil.

Once the altar is consecrated, it should be moved into its position within your sacred space. If it is to be transportable, find a spot where it can be kept safe between castings and workings, remembering that it is a magickal tool and should be treated as such.

Once the altar is consecrated, it should only be used for its intended purpose as stated during the consecration rite, if it is used for any other reason, it is considered desecrated and will require a repeated cleansing and consecration.

A permanent altar may be frequently used depending on the Witch's practice, but should never be allowed to gather dust. A dusty altar is a stagnant altar; the state of such directly reflects the condition of the Craft and the Witch that established it.

You may choose to keep your magickal tools within or upon the altar, both are acceptable practices depending on the Witch's motivation behind the behavior, so be sure to contemplate your purpose for such actions.

The last step is to record in your journal the date and time you set your altar. Be sure to include the location within your sacred space with a brief description, sketch, or photo, along with your thoughts and feelings about your new altar.

Exercise: Programming the Key

For this exercise you will need at least one skeleton key, but if you are drawn to another type of key, use that one instead. I encourage you to seek out a key that you resonate with, whether due to its aesthetic, or the sensation of energy as you hold it in your hand.

The exercise works best if the key you are going to program was originally manufactured as a functioning key, meaning that at one time it actually opened a specific lock, instead of one that is blank and has yet to be keyed, or was made for decorative purposes only, but as with all tools within your Craft, if you are drawn to a specific key, you should use it.

Cleanse the key.

After cleansing, while holding the key in your receptive hand, enter your trance state, and journey to your desired location in the Unseen Realms.

Spend time at the destination, allowing the energy of the frequency to flow through your body and into the key, imbuing it with the energy of this place you've chosen and intend to visit often.

Envision the physical lock that matches the key that you are currently holding. If the key opens a locked door, envision the door in as much detail as possible; if the key opens a padlock, envision that padlock with as much detail as possible.

Visualize yourself putting the key that you're holding into the lock and unlocking the door or padlock.

Now assign this particular key to that specific lock.

Allow this visualization to take as much time as necessary. There is no need to hurry. The more detail you can include during the visualization process, the more successful the program will be.

Before you leave the location, be sure to lock it with your key. The key will not only unlock this specific location, it will also protect it from other travelers and unwanted spirits and entities.

When you return to your conscious state at to the present time from your trance, you should consecrate the key with the purpose of Astral Traveling to that specific location in the Unseen Realms.

Keep the key in a safe place.

This exercise can be done for more than one key, but only one key should be programmed at a time.

Remember to record the experience in your journal; note the date, time, and any other conditions within your environment or within yourself that may have influenced the experience. Record a description or sketch of the key and the location it opens.

Chapter 10

As Above, So Below

Witchcraft includes a knowledge and understanding of correspondences and energetic associations between things, people, and places, so it should not be surprising to find a chapter dedicated to the topic in a book such as this. As you attempt to get *"back to the basics"* of your practice and strengthen your foundation in the basic concepts of Witchcraft and magick, revisiting this topic is a necessity.

"As within, so without; as above, so below"; the macrocosm (universe) influences the microcosm (little world). The Witch knows that nothing is truly separate or distinct from another because everything is part of the interconnection of energy that binds all reality, but we do recognize that some things are more connected than others through their energetic patterns or common elements. With our skills we use these connections to harness the energy in order to manipulate it and manifest our desire into the shared physical reality.

The concept of correspondences has been around

for at least a thousand years and can be traced back to The Doctrine of Signatures, which states that herbs resembling parts of the body can be used to treat ailments that originate in those body parts. The doctrine considers the shape, color, appearance, and number of petals and leaves of a plant, to make a determination as to what the particular plant is able to do for the body or how it will interact with the environment.

Hermeticism, esoteric teachings, and other spiritual paths have also influenced our current use of correspondences within Witchcraft and other magickal practices, and while their use is not necessary for the manifestation of a magickal working, they do allow the Witch to fine tune the energetic vibration of the spell's intention, bringing it closer into resonance with the desired outcome. Since magick takes the path of least resistance, anything that aids the Witch in creating a clearer path from desire to manifestation, or a more powerful alignment between intention and outcome, would be foolish to dismiss without consideration.

There is an appreciation for traditional correspondences that have been used by the Witches of years passed, and it would be prudent for the modern Witch to consult these correspondences before rejecting them solely based on the fact that they are considered traditional. There is a well of energy imbued in these correspondences that today's Witch is able to align with and siphon power from for her or his own spell casting and magickal workings.

For example, ObsidianFire is a modern solitary Witch and she is looking to craft an incense to ease her anxiety about the current state of the world. While discussing her magickal plans with her Witch friend,

BlackStar, who is a hereditary Witch, he shared with her that his Grandmother would often use an old family recipe for a tincture that included Lavender, Chamomile, and Meadowsweet. Now, if ObsidianFire used that same tincture recipe, she would be aligning her own power with not only the energies of those specific herbs, but also with that of BlackStar's Grandmother, who had used the same herbs for the same intention within her own Witchcraft. Those particular herbs were used in the same way and for the same purpose, not only by BlackStar's Grandmother, but also since it was an old family recipe, by all the Witches of that hereditary line, so that ObsidianFire would be joining her magick with the energy stream that was previously established and fed by every other Witch in that bloodline who used those same herbs in the same manner over the years. The well of energy or the specific energy frequency that ObsidianFire would be tapping into and using within her own Witchcraft would be more powerful than if she relied on her own power. This doesn't negate ObsidianFire's own magick or skill, she would most certainly be able to create a tincture of her own that would be successful, but when using an established power, manifestation can occur sooner and / or with more force. This is the power of traditional correspondences.

Not all traditional correspondences are outdated, but they should definitely be regarded within the context of when they were written and practiced. It's beneficial for the Witch to recognize, understand, and know how to interpret the information, and either discard it or incorporate that knowledge into her or his own Craft. Not all shared correspondences will be relevant and sometimes they may not hold true. The

Witch may find that a traditional correspondence for one particular herb found in a spell book or an online source aligns effectively with the desired outcome of a spell casting, but for another magickal working it will not. This doesn't mean that there is something inherently "wrong" with that correspondence table or online source, it simply means that the Witch must work to find a different correspondence that will align better for that spell casting or magickal working.

There are definite benefits with using traditional correspondences, but there are also good reasons for using your own. I encourage the Witch to experiment with both. You will not find correspondence tables in this book as I believe there are plenty of resources available both online and within the pages of published books written for this sole purpose, but what I will include is some of my own reasons for using specific categories of correspondences within my own Witchcraft.

Colors

Color is the quality of an object with respect to light waves that are reflected by the object and is determined visually by the measurement of hue, saturation, and brightness of the reflected light. Human beings are able to perceive color through their sense of sight. The ability to see color is dependent upon the structure of the eye and the light waves that are reflected by objects within the environment.

There are millions of colors within the light spectrum and each color possesses its own energetic vibration. Some of these vibrations will interfere with others, and some will interact with others, but they all have the ability to gain or lose energy in finite amounts related to their vibrational frequency. This energy will never completely die, but will instead continue to exist eternally.

Color is something that I experience daily, so for me it is a common correspondence I use in my Witchcraft, especially when I am working with candle magick. I keep a number of small chime candles in the basic colors of: pink, red, orange, yellow, green blue, purple, black, and white on hand as I find most, if not all, of the intentions I cast for, I associate with one of these colors. This is not to say that candle magick is the only area in which I will use color correspondences, but it is the most frequent.

Any time I craft a charm bag or construct a spell bottle, I will add something of a specific color that corresponds with the intention, if the pouch or bottle itself isn't of the corresponding color. Yarn, twine, fabric, blankets, paper, and ink are other items with which I will use color correspondences.

Herbs, Spices, and Resins

Herbs are the green leaf or flower of a plant with aromatic characteristics that are used to flavor food, make teas, or used as natural medicines. All other elements of the plant, the seeds, buds, bark, that are culinarily used are considered a spice and are usually dried. Human beings have been using herbs and spices for thousands of years and in numerous cultures for a variety of purposes other than to flavor their meals.

Resins are the dried plant secretions. The plant, if injured, will secrete a resin to protect the wound from outside pathogens, like a liquid bandage. These secretions have been valued by humans over the years and have been used for varnishes, adhesives, incense, and perfumes.

Herbs, spices, and resins have been used within many religions and spiritual paths for cleansings, purifications, and other ritualistic purposes. Basil, Cannabis, Cedar, Hemp, Mistletoe, Mugwort, Sweetgrass, Turmeric, Valerian, Vervain, White Sage, Wormwood, and Yarrow; all can be traced to spiritual usage within a tradition or religious practice from ancient to modern times.

Along with color, I most often use herb, spice, and resin correspondences within my Witchcraft. I think it's due to my acute sense of smell and emotional connections I have to aromas. Fresh cut grass, campfires, the air right before it rains, laundry that has been hung out to dry; for me all these smells call to mind memories filled with emotion, which is why I find using the energy of burning herbs powerful within my own practice. If I am able to experience the aroma of an herb, spice, or resin, and connect it energetically to an intention, then I am more easily able to slip into a visualization, which is paramount to casting my spell or working my magick.

I possess a modest collection of herbs, spices, and resins that I use most frequently; among them are: Mugwort, Mullein, Wormwood, Patchouli, Lavender, Rosemary, and Dragon's Blood. I do use others, but these seem to be my favorite.

Hours and Days

Human beings have structured their lives in a linear fashion and have denoted the passing of time in an organization of hours and days, each possessing a specific unique energy that is available to the Witch for use within a spell casting or magickal working. Each hour and day align with a planet or astronomical body in the heavens; the Sun, the Moon, and the planets of Mars, Mercury, Jupiter, Venus, and Saturn.

The planetary hours are based on an ancient astrological system, which assigns one of the astronomical bodies to the hour beginning with Saturn, followed by Jupiter, Mars, the Sun, Venus, Mercury, and the Moon. This order continuously cycles throughout the day. It's important to note, however, that the planetary hours are not the same as the sixty-minute hours that are used for common timekeeping, instead they are divided into twenty-four hours with the first hour of the day beginning with sunrise and the last hour of that same day ending with the sunrise of the next day. Using this system, the length of the day will be varied depending on the season and location of the Witch on the planet.

The astronomical body that rules the first hour of each day is also the one that aligns with the entire day. For example, the first hour of Friday is ruled by Venus, thus making the entire day Venus' day; the first hour of Monday is ruled by the Moon, thus making the entire day Moon's day. This is the origin of the familiar days' names, though most were labeled in Latin and later changed to bear the names of Norse gods; Tuesday is Týr's day, (god of war, law, and justice), Wednesday is Wōden's day, (the "All-Father", possessing a long list of attributes), Thursday is Thor's day, (god of thunder, lightning, and storms), and Friday is Frigg's day, (goddess of wisdom, foresight, and consort to Odin). Saturday, Sunday, and Monday retained their references to the planetary body that ruled the day.

I tend to perform most of my spell castings and

magickal workings after the Sun has set, during the full or dark Moon, so I tend to overlook the day of the week as a correspondence to incorporate in my magick, but if I know that I will be casting during the daytime I tend to prefer to work with the energies of the noontime Sun since it occurs more often during any given month than the full or dark Moon appears.

I have at times, when mundane responsibilities and obligations were of no concern, consulted the planetary hours to determine a more energetically aligned time to cast my spell, and have found in doing so the energy of the hour and day did add power to the casting. When I do consult the planetary hours, I use a free planetary hours astrology program called ChronosXP. It runs from the system tray of Windows where it displays a glyph corresponding to the current planetary hour in any time and or location you choose. A free download is available through multiple hosts and is easily located through an online search.

Lunar Cycle

The lunar phases of new, waxing, full, waning, and dark are created by the changing positions of the Earth, the Moon, and the Sun as the Moon orbits the Earth. It takes the Moon approximately twenty-nine days to complete a lunation or lunar cycle. This is not a precise calculation due to the varying distance between the Moon and the Earth as the Moon orbits around the Earth and the Earth orbits around the Sun.

There are times during the year when the Earth, Moon, and Sun come into perfect alignment, creating a solar eclipse, when the Moon blocks the Sun, which only happens during the new and dark Moon phases, or a lunar eclipse, when the Earth casts a shadow on the Moon, which can only happen during the full Moon phase, but these are uncommon and rare occurrences.

The energy of all lunar phases is available to the Witch that desires to harness it for their Craft, and I most frequently use the energies of the full and dark Moon phases because I find that they are the most potent for drawing or attracting energies and banishing or repelling energies. My spell castings and magickal workings generally can be categorized by one of these two labels.

I want to point out that I perceive a difference between the dark Moon phase and the new Moon phase, even though when we look to the night sky during both phases, it appears as if the Moon is absent. The energy of each phase feels different to me, and so I use them accordingly. The dark Moon phase feels severe, coarse, lethargic, and suspended, while the new Moon phase I perceive as accepting, soothing, eager, and refreshing.

If I am working on a long-term spell or long-term magickal working, then I generally begin the casting on either the dark Moon or full Moon phase and continuously work the magick for the full lunation, ending on the phase in which I began.

Blood

Blood is the fluid that delivers necessary nutrients and oxygen to the cells of the physical body; without blood the body would die. It is due to the importance of blood, and the genetic connection to the body in which it was produced, that it is used within Witchcraft. The fluid holds a strong energetic bond, not only to the owner, but to life itself, and because of this bond, when blood is used within a spell, it binds the owner to the intention of the working, whether or not the owner is aware of what is transpiring.

Using other fluids (semen, tears, saliva, urine) and parts of the physical body (hair, eyelashes, nail clippings, teeth, solid waste) will also bind the owner to the intention of the spell, but nothing is as powerful as blood due to its nature and importance to life. The Witch requires only a few drops, even flakes of dried blood, as it also carries the same energetic vibration.

Blood is a correspondence that I use because of the vitality and power it holds, although it is not a personal common correspondence. I use blood only for important or more serious spells or magickal workings that I feel require a binding; either of my energy to the intention or to the target.

Exercise: Working with Correspondences

Take a few moments to read the following scenarios and consider whether the correspondences presented within each example are the same ones that you might use if you were to cast the spell or do the magickal working suggested. In your journal, note the intention of each suggested spell or magickal working, along with the correspondences that were given and those that you would choose instead, if there is a difference, along with your reasons for selecting the alternative ones you've chosen.

Keep in mind while you are doing this exercise that there are no "right" or "wrong" answers. This is only an opportunity for you to consider how you might work correspondences into your own spell castings and magickal workings. At the end of this chapter you will find my choices along with my personal reasons for choosing those particular correspondences.

1. Holly lost the keys to her old apartment and her ex-boyfriend wanted them back, which meant she needed to find them quick. Along with looking for them in all the usual places, she decided to cast a spell to aid her with the task. There was a waning Moon occurring that night, which she decided was the perfect Moon phase for her spell. She gathered the required ingredients: a silver candle, Spearmint essential oil, and an incense mix she crafted with Patchouli, Catnip, and Cedar.

2. Unhappy with his current job, Mirage decided to find himself a new position somewhere else. While submitting numerous applications and resumes, he also decided to craft a spell to help him find new employment, after all what was magick for if not to use it, right? There was a waxing Moon happening and he was ready to harness its energy. He decided to

print out a blank job application and fill it out in red ink, then he would anoint the paper application with Patchouli essential oil and burn it in his cauldron with a handful of Mullein, Sandalwood, and Vervain, while reciting the incantation he had written.

3. Oleander's mother was experiencing some medical issues after being involved in a car accident. He believed that her healing would be accelerated with some help of the energetic sort. He planned to hold a healing session on the night of the full Moon and would be incorporating a black-colored blanket, an oil crafted with Jasmine essential oil, and an incense made of Rosebuds, Chamomile, and Dittany of Crete.

4. StormHawk had been single since he and his boyfriend of five years broke-up over a year ago and he was tired of being alone. He had downloaded a few dating apps, and signed up for some online dating services, but felt that, with a little magickal boost, he might just find the love he was searching for, someone with whom he could spend the rest of his life. There was a new Moon happening on Sunday night and he felt that he was ready to cast a spell. He decided that he was going to use three blue candles, each anointed with Neroli essential oil, a piece of parchment paper, a red inked pen, and an incense mix crafted from Mandrake, Wormwood, and Lavender.

5. There was a spirit in ObsidianFire's home

causing all sorts of chaos. After some cautious magickal investigation, she discovered that the spirit was attached to a wardrobe that her husband recently purchased from an antique shop. There was no doubt that this spirit needed to be released from the wardrobe and banished from their home. On Wednesday night, under the gaze of the dark Moon, she performed her magick. She cleansed the wardrobe with a wash she brewed of distilled water and Black Pepper. She anointed a black candle with Juniper essential oil, and after securing it in a candle holder, she lit it, and placed it on top of the wardrobe. While the candle burned, she mixed together Lilac, Cloves, Frankincense, and Myrrh, and burned it in her cauldron as she cast her spell.

Exercise: Moon Cycle Chart

In your journal, using the chart on the next page, or one similar to it, note the energy you feel within yourself and in your environment the day prior to, the day of, and the day after each Moon phase. Begin with either the coming new or full Moon and continue until the dark Moon. It may be beneficial to chart for numerous lunar cycles.

By charting the energy you experience during each Moon phase, you will be able to determine which one would best correspond with the intention of your spells and magickal workings.

An example entry is filled in for you as a guide.

Moon Cycle Chart

Day Prior	Day of Phase	Day After
Date: *April 22*	New	
Excited, alert, aware, Anticipating, alive	*Excited, active, happy, Chaotic, vibrant*	*Alive, vibrating, joy, Expectant, shifting*
Date:	Waxing	
Date	Full	
Date	Waning	
Date:	Dark	
Date:	New	
Date:	Waxing	
Date:	Full	
Date:	Waning	
Date:	Dark	

My Choices for the Correspondence Exercise:

1. The intention for this spell is to relocate lost keys, so I would do the spell during a waxing Moon, not waning, because I want to build the energy, not lessen it. A silver candle is good if I am using primordial feminine energies, but I would rather siphon aggressive energies for seeking something out, so I would choose an orange candle. Spearmint essential oil is used for stimulating mental powers, so I would use it, but I would not use that incense mix. Instead I would replace the Patchouli with Sage since Patchouli is an herb that I would use for money or fertility and things of that nature, while Sage is an herb that I would use for granting wishes, and I wish to find the key. Catnip corresponds with happiness, so I would keep that since finding the lost key would bring me joy, but I would replace the Cedar with Allspice, since Cedar is more aligned with purification and protection and I'm looking for luck, which aligns better with the energy of Allspice.

2. The intention of this spell is to find a job. The waxing Moon's energy is good for this. Filling out a job application is a great idea, however I would use green ink to correspond with money instead of red, and anointing the application with Patchouli essential oil is perfect. Since I love Patchouli, I would continue using it and burn it in the cauldron with a handful of Basil instead of the Mullein,

which I tend to associate with spirit work, Sandalwood, for wishes, and Vervain, for money.

3. The intention of this spell is healing. The full Moon is definitely a workable phase for almost all spells and magickal healings, so I would agree with this correspondence, but I would use either a white or blue blanket, blue being associated with healing, instead of the black one, which I associated with protection. The Jasmine essential oil, since it is aligned with love energy, is a valid choice, however I would prefer to use Carnation, which aligns with protection, strength, and healing. The incense made of Rosebuds, Chamomile, and Dittany of Crete, I would change to Rosebuds, for love and healing; Cinnamon, for success and healing; and St. John's Wort, for health and strength. Chamomile is usually associated with sleep and Dittany of Crete is used for spirit work and astral projection.

4. The intention of this spell is to find a lover. The new Moon phase is acceptable for new beginnings, but I personally would choose the full Moon, for heart's desire, and I would choose Friday, being the day of Venus or Frigg, both associated with love, and not Sunday, which is associated with the Sun. I would opt for two red candles instead of the three blue ones, since blue for me tends to be healing, while red is love or lust. The Neroli essential oil is a perfect choice as it aligns with love. The incense mix crafted from

Mandrake, Wormwood, and Lavender is not a combination that I would usually consider using for a love spell, but it does align well with the intention. While Lavender is a flower that I do associate with love, Mandrake is an herb I use for fertility, and Wormwood for spells dealing with psychic powers and calling spirits.

5. The intention for this spell is exorcism and banishment of a spirit. In my opinion, the timing of the spell being Wednesday during a dark Moon is a good choice. The wash she made works for me as well. Black Pepper as well as Red Pepper are aligned with exorcism. Anointing a black candle with Juniper essential oil corresponds with the intention of the spell, as does the incense mix of Lilac, Cloves, Frankincense, and Myrrh.

Chapter 11

Spell Crafting and Casting

Every human being has the ability to create energetic changes within their life, and each of us are able to use the influences of our environments to achieve this goal. This idea is the basic concept of magick. Each individual is the creator of their own life experience and if, as Witch, we encounter something we don't like or don't want, we recognize and acknowledge that we hold the power to make a change in our mundane reality with the aid of Witchcraft. This step in getting *"back to the basics"* of our Craft covers how we make the changes we seek to manifest in our lives.

Witchcraft is the craft of a Witch and is as unique as the Witch who practices it. There is no one way or "right" way to practice Witchcraft, but most importantly it is a practice, an action, and an act of Will. Witchcraft requires knowledge and understanding of magick; both high magick (theurgy) and low magick (thaumaturgy). It is a skill that requires dexterity and aptitude, and while it can be taught, not everyone is capable of practicing, because not everyone is meant to be Witch.

Once an individual accepts that they are Witch, it is something they are every day of their lives; it isn't an identity they adopt on All Hallow's Eve. It isn't the black velvet hooded cloak they purchased in Salem, Massachusetts, last year to be worn only during their full Moon rituals. Witch is who they are and who they are becoming at their core; it is how they live, how they think, act, and speak. Witch isn't something that an individual can separate from her or himself because it is the self.

A Witch is someone who is aware of their own energy, as well as the energies surrounding them at any given moment, regardless of where it originates, and is able to align with and siphon those energies for the purpose of working magick. The Witch, through seeking and studying, has established a relationship with both the Physical and Unseen Realms of existence, both the forces of nature and the spirits, and will use their innate psychic abilities to practice: conjuration, divination, dowsing, prophecy, remote viewing, astral projection, and scrying. Though not all Witches will do all these things, many of them will. A Witch embraces their abilities, skills, and power, and owns it all without fear, but with confidence.

The ability to sense and manipulate magick doesn't just leave the Witch or fade away. Witchcraft, once it is acknowledged and accepted, is never lost, because it is something that the Witch does; it is an activity, a perception of this reality and all others. It is all the actions that the Witch purposefully chooses to do or not do. In the process of becoming Witch, the individual's Witchcraft may shift focus depending on what the individual is experiencing in life.

For example, let's say that our friend, BlackStar,

in the month of August, was dealing with neighbor drama, so he focused his magick solely with the intention of protection. He crafted amulets for his family members, summoned his familiar spirits to ward their home, enchanted mirrors and placed them in the house windows, set up a crystal grid in the yard, and crafted a Witch's Bottle, burying it on the property. BlackStar's focus was on protection the entire month.

In September, his mother fell ill, and since he was a Reiki Master, he shifted his focus from protection to healing, and spent his time sending distance Reiki to his mother, as well as doing Reiki sessions with her when he visited in person. He searched out simple herbal remedies to offer her and crafted healing bath salts for her to use.

When October arrived, BlackStar spent the majority of his time communing with his Beloved Dead and preparing for All Hallow's Eve. During the month he didn't do much spell casting, but spent time practicing divination of all types, even learning how to cast bones.

In November, our Witch friend spent his time working on his own Shadows, as he had experienced some conflict with another one of our friends, which brought up some of his own personal challenges and issues. Instead of doing a lot of spell crafting or casting, he spent plenty of time in contemplation and journaling.

He realized during this time he really needed time to focus on self-care, which he did during the month of December. The only other thing he spent his time on was celebrating the Winter Solstice with us and a few of our other Witch friends.

In January, BlackStar found that he wanted to

spend more time meditating and working with energy, so he restarted his Yoga and Tai Chi practice, but again he didn't spend a lot of time spell casting.

As February approached, he realized that he would benefit from an influx of cash, so he began crafting and casting money spells to bring in some prosperity.

This example is one of a varied magickal practice, but it's no doubt Witchcraft. The months that our Witchy friend, BlackStar, didn't cast spells or craft incense or commune with the spirits, he was still practicing his Craft.

Calling yourself Witch doesn't make you Witch, but understanding that every action you make is magickal at its core, does. It is our perception that transforms even mundane tasks into something magickal in its nature. A morning shower isn't just washing the body, with conscious intention it's an act of complete purification of the body, mind, and spirit, because when a seemingly mundane physical task is accompanied by a visualization and fueled with emotions, the Witch is able to propel the intention of purification into reality. Getting dressed each day, drinking that first cup of morning coffee, driving to work, these and every other deliberate mundane act, when directed by the Witch's Will and powered by her or his emotions, is an act of magick.

The definition of a spell is the conscious and deliberate, specific attempt, ideally a successful one, to harness and manipulate energy through Will and emotions, following a formula crafted by the Witch in order to achieve an outcome within the Witch's reality.

Casting the spell is an action. It is the process of taking the conscious and deliberate, specific attempt, in the form of a thought, which is birthed in the Unseen Realm, and manifesting it into the Physical Realm. Spells may be cast in different ways. All of the following activities are forms of spell casting when done by the Witch:

- brewing potions, elixirs, infusions, tinctures
- creating ointments, salves, and oils
- mixing herbs for incense and bath salts
- sewing poppets and hex or charm bags
- making candles and dressing them
- tying knots
- molding and sculpting clay
- drawing or painting a picture
- writing poetry
- dancing
- singing
- cooking
- sex

It is impossible to be Witch without casting spells, unless your practice consists of solely performing magickal workings.

A magickal working is similar to a spell, but commonly doesn't include a formula to be followed by the Witch. A working may be more spontaneous in nature and not require any corresponding ingredients, though actions are still required, as described in the term itself, "magickal working", the word "work" indicates physical sustained effort and / or action. For example, healings, such as laying of hands, and acts of sex magick, may be referred to as magickal workings.

There are numerous books and websites overflowing with spells written by Witches, both famous and unknown, available to the novice and sage Witch alike, but it is more beneficial for the Witch to write and cast her or his own spells regardless of the celebrity status of the published Witch's spell. This is not to infer that the printed spells are more or less powerful than something the novice Witch might craft for themselves, nor should those spells be considered outdated or fake. The suggestion that a Witch should craft her or his own spells is primarily due to the fact that, when the Witch puts personal time and effort into crafting the spell, it will align the intention of the spell with the energy of the Witch crafting it, and therefore will provide the spell with more power and chance for success than someone else's spell, which will carry their energy. If the Witch does decide to use a spell that she or he found in a book or online, then I suggest that for the intention of the spell to successfully manifest, it is vital that the Witch completely understand the reasoning behind using the provided correspondences, and to know and comprehend the meaning of the words written in the incantation. It would also be prudent for the Witch to "make it their own", meaning that she or he should include a personal correspondence, a phrase, or gesture in the already crafted spell to ensure that they have invested something of their own energy into the spell.

Every successful spell includes the components: the Witch, a target, an intention, power, and Will. Many spells will also include some form of words and correspondences that align with the intention, and there usually is some sort of order as to how the spell is cast, which may be spontaneous or planned in a ritualistic structure, but there are always physical actions to be done by the Witch. Spell casting isn't about stillness. It isn't about doing nothing except thinking. It's about doing something.

Spell casting and magickal workings are activities that require actual physical mundane movements. For a spell or magickal working to manifest, the Witch must exert effort to create and birth the desired change. Both are actions of mind and body through the work of spirit, and if the Witch is not engaging all aspects of the self, then that individual is not working magick, regardless of what she or he believes or labels it. When dwelling in the realm of physical matter, physical actions are required for manifestation; unless, of course, you are a Witch who has reached such an evolved level of being that you are beyond the physicality of this realm, and while I mean no offense to any Witch I have met or have yet to meet in this lifetime, I am confident that you have not yet achieved such a state of being.

Witch

Within a spell there must be someone to cast it. The Witch is the magick user, the individual who is self-aware, skillful in achieving the required trance state in order to visualize the intention, and the target, if said target isn't in the presence of the Witch. The Witch possesses the ability to harness the siphoned power so that it can be successfully used to propel the spell towards the target and ultimately towards the desired manifestation.

Target

The target is who or what is to be changed or affected. This might be the Witch, a person the Witch has a relationship with, another human being or animal, a situation or condition within the Witch's life, or a situation or condition that effects the shared reality or the whole of humanity. A target might be as all-encompassing as the planet or as specific as something that will fit in the palm of the Witch's hand.

Intention

The components of intention, power, and Will are intimately connected and interact with each other during a spell casting or magickal working.

Intention is the goal and the steps required to bring about the desired change. It is the idea, the thoughts, and the outcome of the crafted spell or magickal working. It's the change that the Witch desires to manifest into reality. It is, simply, the motive for the spell casting. When the Witch is crafting a spell or planning a magickal working, the first thing that must be considered is the intention, but while intention is vital, it isn't the only component that is required. "Sending out an intention" is not synonymous with spell casting.

For example, BlackStar may sit outside at night beneath the full Moon and consciously decide that he desires to bring prosperity into his life, and while sitting there on the grass underneath the beauty of that night sky, while gazing at the luminescence of the Moon, he devises a plan on how to execute this desire to be prosperous, but this in and of itself, as just described, is not casting a spell. This is just the beginning of the work that is required of BlackStar to bring about prosperity in his life.

Power

Power is the energy that propels the intention towards the target for physical manifestation. It is what builds the momentum within our thoughts, emotions, and actions, including our intentions. Energy can be found not only within the Witch, but is inherent on and in the Earth; it isn't something that we create, it's something that always is, always was, and will always be. It's found within the Unseen Realms, spiritual entities, nature, or surrounding environment, and Universal Source or divinity.

There seems to be a common belief that if the Witch is ill or feeling tired, then spell casting and magickal workings should not be done, because when completed, the Witch will be energetically depleted. This is simply false. Energy is everywhere and there are always power sources available to the Witch that should be used when your own energy is low, or if there is a desire to add or merge your own power with another. The energy from the old Birch tree in your backyard will feel different and hold a different power than your own. The energy from your familiar spirit will enhance your own power for a spell casting. When petitioning for aid from a god or goddess, their power will manifest differently than if you attempted the working with solely your own power. If you feel drained after a casting or working, then you are pulling too heavily on your own energy, and are hindering your own Craft. It would be beneficial to siphon the power from an available outside source.

When raising power, the Witch will benefit from allowing the momentum to grow organically, shifting from a low, slow energy to high, quick energy over a period of time, to be determined by the Witch and the level of her or his own energy at the time of the casting. The moment to release the raised energy and direct it toward the target is the moment just before the energy feels as if it's peaking, because it will take a heartbeat for you to release it. If you wait until the energy peak and then release it, you will be releasing energy that is already dissipating.

There are numerous ways to raise power and not all methods work for everyone, so exploring and experimenting will be important for you to discover which method or methods work best. Chanting is what I use most often, but I will also choose another method if I feel the success of spell I'm casting depends on it. Switching the method of raising power can be beneficial, especially if you're working with another Witch, or if you're attempting to be discreet with the spell casting or magickal working.

If you feel as if there is residual energy swirling or rushing around you within your sacred space after you have cast your spell or completed your magickal working, this is often due to unsuccessfully sending all the raised energy to the designated target. Any energy raised must be focused, brought to a peak, and either sent to a target or returned to its source, if this process is ignored the Witch usually feels overstimulated or exhausted. I have found that excess energy is best transferred back to the Earth, regardless of the original source from which is was siphoned, for absorption in a process known as earthing. Earthing is done by placing the palms of your hands on the ground while visualizing the excess energy from your sacred space being absorbed into your body and spirit, transferred down your arms, through your palms, and into the planet.

Grounding is similar to earthing, but involves the Witch anchoring her or himself to the planet. It is the process in which a two-way channel is established between Witch and Earth, bringing the focus of the Witch back to the Physical Realm and present moment of awareness.

There are a variety of ways to ground oneself, but the method I often use is: I close my eyes, stand with bare feet parallel and about twelve inches apart, though I have practiced grounding with socks and shoes on, inhale deeply through my nose, filling my lungs fully, being sure that my belly rises and falls as I breathe, and exhale through the mouth. I breathe at least three times, more if I feel still feel tension in my body. I then slowly raise my arms until they are above my head with fingers outstretched to the sky, extending my arms and fingers as far as I am able, and then I smile, sometimes I laugh.

Then I begin my visualization: I focus on my center, the fount of personal power, which is located around my diaphragm, and I concentrate on how my body feels in that moment. This process is known as centering, and as I gather my energy from this well, I send it through me, down my torso, through my legs, and out the soles of my feet to connect with the planet, while I also send my energy up my torso, through my shoulders, arms, and out my finger tips to connect with the heavens. I continue the visualization until I sense that, not only is my own energy being sent into the ground beneath my feet and out into the heavens, but that I am also receiving energy from these sources as well, creating the two-way channel and anchoring me to the Physical Realm.

Will

Will is the Witch's own belief, faith, and confidence in her or his own knowledge, ability, and skill with magick. It is the capacity to deliberately choose a course of action, instead of reacting to outside influences. It's the physic function that bridges the Unseen Realms with the Physical Realm. Attempting to cast a spell or do a magickal working without Will would be a waste of time and energy, as it's required to transform an intention into manifestation.

A Witch who decides to cast a spell to heal her or himself of a medical condition that they were diagnosed with must possess the Will and belief that the condition can be changed, or else the spell will never manifest. A shift in perception will never occur as there is no belief in the Witch's own ability to create the change that he or she thought they desired, but the Witch who does possess the Will and belief that the condition can change, and that the condition will not hinder them, that individual has potential for manifesting a change.

For example, ObsidianFire was recently diagnosed with Generalized Anxiety Disorder (GAD) by her physician. She embraces the diagnosis and thinks to herself: "I have GAD, the doctor diagnosed me and now I'm a Witch with GAD and that's just the way it is. I need to accept it and live with it for the rest of my life." Here she identifies herself with the disorder and often refers to herself as anxious: "I am anxious", and with this thought process she is not in a state of willingness. She has created internal resistance to change because she doesn't believe, have faith, or confidence in her ability and skill with magick for the change to manifest.

To read more on the topic of Will and its importance in The Witches' Pyramid, refer back to the previous chapter of this book titled *Magick*.

Words

Words are the incantation, the symbols of the intention, that span all realms of existence; they exist in the Unseen Realms, and once written or spoken, become tangible to the immediate senses, thus manifesting that which didn't previously exist. Each word in any language has a distinct vibrational frequency, whether it is read, written, or spoken. Our voices create an energetic vibration that travels through the air when we speak. Words are thoughts manifested into the Physical Realm.

When crafting a spell it's important to understand the distinction between a need and a want. The words are often used interchangeably, but there's a subtle energetic difference that the Witch shouldn't overlook. The vibration of a spell can easily be shifted, and not always in the most beneficial way, when the word need is used instead of want. Perhaps it's the influence of Christianity that is prevalent throughout our society, which encourages us to be altruistic, and self-sacrificing, to deny our wants and unapologetically condemn those who embrace and revel in our most natural desires, that encourages us to only identify, vocalize, and pursue our needs, while denying our desires because desires are rooted in selfishness. For the Witch who is spell casting or doing a magickal working, wants are exactly what should be emphasized. Each of us are here in the Physical Realm, dwelling in a physical body, living a physical life; we are expected to want things, and as Witch, we have the power to manifest them.

A want is defined as a desire to come, go, or be; in simpler terms, a want is a desire, and a need is a lack of something requisite, desirable, or useful; to put it more simply a need is a lack. The part of the self that is responsible for recognizing what it lacks and what it possesses is the ego. It is focused on the requirements of survival in the Physical Realm of existence and it's constantly ensuring the self that these requirements or needs are met. There is a constant fear within the ego that the needs are not being met and that fear creates resistance within the Witch.

Wants are rooted within the authentic self, a part of each of us that does not fear. It has no concern about what is lacking within the totality of the self, but instead has understanding of the nature of self, the universe, and deity. This is where the Witch finds her or his fount of personal power.

When casting a spell or working magick, if the Witch is focused on a need, there is an emphasis on what is lacking in the target, whether the target is the Witch, another person, thing, condition, or other. There is the perception of emptiness within the target that must be filled. This void then becomes the actual target of the spell, regardless of what or who the Witch perceives the target to be. The energetic frequency that the Witch is aligning with is the lack, even if the Witch states with their words something different.

For example, ObsidianFire casts a money spell which states:

"On this night and in this hour,

I cast this spell with my own power.
Cash and coin is what I need,
Of this debt we shall be freed,
By Water, Fire, Earth, and Air,
I only ask for our fair share.
To buy some food and pay the rent,
All our savings has been spent.
This is my Will, this is my plea,
As I Will it, so mote it be!"

The energetic frequency that ObsidianFire is propelling into the ethers is lack, even though she pronounces that they need the money to buy food and pay the rent, the focus within the spell is a lack of money. They have none, therefore they need some, but if ObsidianFire focused instead on what she wants, then the emphasis would be on what she desires or wishes to manifest in her life. There is no perceived lack, no void to fill, just a desire to bring something in, to add to what is already present. Whatever it is she wishes for, that thing, person, or condition would be the actual target of the spell. The energetic frequency that she would be projecting into the ethers is her desire.

ObsidianFire could reword the spell like this:

"On this night and in this hour,
I cast this spell with my own power,
I want some coin and some cash,
So make it quick, like in a flash.
By Water, Fire, Earth, and Air,
I'm seeking out our fair share.
The cash I see, it does accrue,
And spend it well is what I'll do.
This is my Will, this is my plea,

As I Will it, so mote it be!"

With this rewrite there is no suggestion that ObsidianFire doesn't have money, but rather that she wants it, perhaps even more of it. With the clear understanding that the Witch casts for what she or he desires, there is a focus on the outcome of the spell, not on the present circumstance, which in many cases is one of lack. The momentum of a cast spell is driven by the intensity of the power that fuels the intention towards its designated target, so emphasizing the lack does a hindrance to the casting by creating a greater need for that which is lacking, and is the primary way of sabotaging the spell or magickal working. The Witch that is focused on their want, the power of that desire will build momentum and ultimately manifest it in their life experience.

Correspondences

Correspondences are the items and associations that align with the intention and enable the energy to be brought into alignment, ensuring a greater success rate for the spell. To read more on the topic of correspondences and their importance in spell crafting and casting, refer back to the previous chapter of this book titled *As Above, So Below*.

After the casting of a spell is complete, the Witch should consider what to do with the remnants, if there are any. Remains such as ashes, candle wax, bits of paper, or food, should be treated as important as all other elements of the spell or magickal working. These remaining fragments hold the energy of the spell's intention, and what the Witch decides to do with them will affect the alignment of the intention's energy and ultimately the outcome of the spell. It's vital that the Witch contemplate what she or he will do with the remains prior to the casting so that hasty, impulsive actions are not taken after the work is completed.

For example, if ObsidianFire flushed the remains of her prosperity spell down the toilet, this would not be in alignment with the intention of attracting cash and coin into her purse, instead it holds the opposing energy; to rid herself of prosperity. A better option for ObsidianFire is to bury the remnants as if planting a seed or wrapping up the remains, if they are small enough, and keeping them in her wallet. There are plenty of options that are in alignment with the intention of your spell, so contemplate and choose wisely.

Suspending, Recalling, and Reversing a Spell

Once a spell is cast, the energy, which is in motion, will continue to build momentum until an outcome is manifested in the Physical Realm. This concept is supported by Sir Isaac Newton's First Law of Motion, which states:

"Every object persists in its state of rest or uniform motion in a straight line unless it is compelled to change that state by forces impressed on it."

The cast spell will move towards its target with the same power and in the same direction as it was originally cast unless the intention is acted upon by an unstable or outside force. In most circumstances, once a spell is cast and the magick is released towards its intended target, it cannot be stopped or recalled, unless there are instances present that allow for a suspension, a recall, a reversal, or arrest. This is something that the Witch is able to do when crafting a spell by writing in a specified time-frame or trigger within the incantation.

Here's an example of an incantation for a spell that includes a specific time-frame:

"I cast this spell on this night,
Underneath the full Moon's sight.
Wealth abundant please do share,
By the element of air.
Flowing cash is what I want,
Manifest a flowing font.
Before the last day comes to pass,
Make it quick and make it last.
This is my Will, this is my plea.
As I Will it, so shall it be!"

The wording of this particular spell states that the cash should manifest before the last day and that it should be quick. If the Witch wanted to stop this spell once it was cast, it would be a difficult task due to the time-frame and force of the intention.

Here's an example of an incantation for a spell that includes a trigger:

"I cast this spell on this night,
Beneath Circe's keen eye sight.
With her wisdom I do cast,
This magick is right, strong, and fast.
Send to me a lover true,
With hair of brown and eyes of blue.
A quick wit, a handsome face,

Steady job, expensive taste,
Tall and slender, charming, too,
A voice of honey with which to woo.
On my thirty-first birthday,
And with hardly a word to say,
He will walk into my life,
And I will be his faithful wife.
This is my Will, this is my plea,
As I Will it, so mote it be!"

The wording of this particular spell sets the trigger as the thirty-first birthday, suggesting that even though this spell might be cast while the Witch was nineteen, the spell will not manifest until she reached her thirty-first birthday. This would be an easier spell to stop due to the trigger, especially if the spell was cast many years prior to the actual trigger date as this would gain the Witch the time to build a momentum of energy or force with which to stop the original spell.

Ideally, if the Witch has taken the required time to prepare, she or he should not be concerned about suspending, recalling, reversing, or stopping a spell once it's cast. I find that it's best to allow all spell castings and magickal workings to take their course and manifest into the Physical Realm, even if I have begun to second guess and question my actions.

Failure to Manifest

The most frustrating situation for the Witch to encounter within their Craft is when a cast spell or magickal working fails to manifest. There are multiple reasons as to why this occurs, many of which can be rectified.

The first step is to consider whether you, as Witch, were able to shift your perception of the target during visualization. As discussed in the second chapter titled *Altered States*, it is vital for the Witch to be able to experience a desired changed within a trance state before being able to experience it in the Physical Realm. It is the way in which that desired change becomes a reality. If the Witch is unable to visualize and experience the change in the Astral Realm, then it will never manifest in the Physical Realm. It would benefit you to take time to contemplate your beliefs and fears concerning the intention of your spell or magickal working, as it is possible that you are personally stopping the manifestation from occurring due to your beliefs and / or any fears you may be harboring.

The next consideration is your ability to focus and concentrate while casting your spell or working your magick, as both are necessary. The Witch that loses focus or concentration will inevitably affect the outcome and the intention will not manifest. Being in sacred space, feeling comfortable with yourself and the work at hand, ensuring that there is no possibility of interruptions during the casting or working, and having all the required ingredients, tools, and items for your Craft, will ensure that you will be focused on what is required. There is nothing worse than being in the moment and feeling the energy aligning with your spell only to be interrupted by your cell phone.

The Will of the Witch should also be considered when an intention fails to manifest. If the current energetic momentum of the target is greater than that of the Witch, the cast spell or magickal working will not manifest. The force of power that was used to cast or do the working should be contemplated. If there is an intention directed towards a target that is weaker than the Will of the target, or the condition influencing or surrounding the target, then the likelihood of the cast spell affecting the target is slight. In order to create the desired change, the Witch would be required to build a power greater than that which is being created and held by the target. The Will of the Witch must be stronger than the Will of the target. It would be more effective for you to cast a spell negating the current intention of the target, or the condition influencing the target, than attempting to completely change it. It's easier to force something off its set course than to completely reverse its direction.

You should also consider whether you are simply being impatient. The impatient Witch may seek to recast a spell when it's unnecessary as the intention has not yet manifested or manifestation has occurred, but the Witch is ignorant of the outcome. The time required for a cast spell or magickal working to manifest will differ greatly from Witch to Witch and situation to situation. Because magick takes the path of least resistance, the span of time that will pass before manifestation occurs is never a guarantee. When you work mundanely in accordance with the intention of your cast spell, or magickal working, removing any obstacles that may be hindering the manifestation and working to release any energetic blockages that may be restraining the magick, you will always be encouraging a quicker manifestation.

Lastly there are instances when you may be unaware that your cast spell successfully manifested, because the expectation as to how it would manifest and the reality of how it did are not one and the same. When you consider your spells and magickal workings, you should keep in mind that there are no such things as coincidences or synchronicities. Your experiences are the result of your magick. Just because the spell did not manifest in the exact way you visualized and intended, doesn't mean it did not manifest at all. Understanding the first power within The Witches' Pyramid will enable you to recognize the manifestations of your spells and workings easier and with more success.

It took me years of honest (and sometimes brutal) personal reflection and Shadow Work to be able to recognize the ways in which I sabotage my own Witchcraft. I am Witch, and as such, I am aware that there is no outside force to blame for the failures of my cast spells or magickal workings. If an outcome didn't manifest, it's on me, just as it's my success when it does. This is my Craft. I'm the one that is accountable. I claim responsibility. No one "made me do it". I did it of my own accord. This gnosis leads to my understanding that there are always reasons for the results of my magick. It just sometimes takes me a while to accept it. I'm quick to berate myself for failures, so I make a sincere effort to uncover any obvious signs, coincidences, and synchronicities that I've been successful in order to validate my work.

I know that I tend to be impatient. I cast a spell tonight, and as the sun rises, I want to see that the change already occurred, but more often than not, the change I desire will happen over the following days or weeks – sometimes even months. The time span required for that change to occur grows exponentially with the influence, significance, and strength of that which I desire to change.

Exercise: Imbuing Energy

It's possible to imbue an item, a tool, or symbol with intention and focus. This power will be accumulated within the item, tool, or symbol over a span of time, allowing the Witch, or other individual, to access the collected power at a later date, however that person would still require concentration and focus to access the stored power.

For this exercise you will need a physical item, tool or symbol, and an emotion you will work with to build the energy that you will be powering the chosen item. I suggest selecting an item that you associate with the emotional energy you will be raising. For example, if I decide to work with the emotion of joy or happiness, then imbuing that energy into a smiley face necklace is an understandable choice, but imbuing the joy or happiness into a skull ring may not be a common association. Choose your item and emotion wisely and be sure the association works for you, or the individual you may be gifting the item, tool, or symbol.

I encourage you to choose the emotion that is most prominent with you in the moment that you decide to do the exercise as it will be the easiest for you to access, and it would be best for you to read this entire exercise before attempting it.

After reading through the rest of the exercise, enter your trance state in whatever way you have successfully done with the previous exercises, and once you're there, fully embrace the emotion you decided to use.

Allow the feelings to rise within you and slowly overwhelm you. During this experience, if you feel compelled to move, then you should move. You may want to dance, stomp, rock, clap, shout, or a combination of movements. Don't second guess yourself, and whatever you feel compelled to do, do it! Fully immerse yourself in the emotional energy as it rises within you and aligns with your own power.

Once you feel as if you are one with the emotion, clap then rub your hands together briskly a few times to activate your palms.

Grasp your chosen item in your dominate hand. If the item is too large or too heavy, then hold it with both hands.

Visualize the energy you have raised within you as a ball, similar to the one you created in the previous exercises: *Energy Ball* and *Energy Ball Revisited.* The color of this energy ball will most likely organically correspond with the type of emotion you used, or some shade of your own energy, as it is part of your essence. Take time with the visualization, allowing it to unfold in real time. If you are able to visualize with your eyes open, do so as this is the preferred method.

Now slowly move this raised energy ball from your fount of power, located somewhere within your torso, and direct it down your upper arm(s), slowly along your forearm(s), down to your wrist(s), and into your hand(s). Be sure to proceed at a very slow pace as you concentrate on the movement of energy through your body. Moving the energy too quickly will fragment your focus and the energy will dissipate within your body. If this does happen, start the exercise again from the beginning step at raising the emotional energy.

Allow the energy ball to gradually seep out of your palm(s) and into the item you are holding.

Take time projecting the energy into the item and continue the process until you no longer feel the energy surging within your body.

This item now holds your raised emotional energy, which you or someone else can use later. It can also be used to power other items or tools, like a battery.

Remember to record the time and date of the magickal working in your journal, along with a description or sketch of the item you imbued and what type of emotional energy you used. Include any notes pertaining to yourself and the environmental conditions surrounding you at the time of the working that may have influenced the outcome.

Exercise: Drawing Energy

It's possible and recommended for the Witch, when her or his personal energy is depleted, or when a spell casting or magickal working calls for it, to draw energy from an item, another living being, including animals, plants, flora, a person or group of people, or a place with conscious intention and focus. This power can be used by the Witch to cast a spell, do a magickal working, including powering a rite or ritual, or to imbue an item.

For this exercise you will need a natural and / or living item such as: a stone, some salt or dirt, bowl of water, a candle flame, or a house plant. I would discourage the use of a living animal, person, or group of people when attempting the exercise for the first time, but once you've mastered this technique, advancing to drawing energy from any of these is suggested.

As with the previous exercises, I encourage you to read through this exercise completely before attempting it.

When ready, clap your hands, then rub them together briskly a few times to activate your palms.

Place your chosen item on a table or other flat

surface in front of you and extend your non-dominate (receptive) hand over the item, or if your chosen item is small enough, hold it in your non-dominate hand.

Next you should enter your trance state in whatever way you have successfully done with the previous exercises, and once you're there, focus on your chosen item with eyes open or closed, though open is the preferred method.

Extend your awareness to include the item so that you're able to sense its energy.

Now visualize the energy flowing as it moves through the object and consider how you would describe it. Is it hot, cold, sharp, smooth? Does it tingle? What color is the energy? How does the energy sound as it flows through the item? Is there an aroma or taste that accompanies the energy?

Shift your focus to the palm of your extended hand or the hand that is holding the item.

Visualize the energy just as you have described it, gathering into an energy ball within the item.

Then with your concentration and focus, pull the energy ball from the item into the palm of your hand. Hear the sounds of the energy, as you draw it from the object, feel the sensation of the energy gathering in your palm, and see the energy converging there.

When the ball of energy is in your hand, hold it for a few moments, concentrating on the sensations you are experiencing.

Then slowly allow it to draw it into your palm so that it permeates your hand.

Now very slowly move the ball of energy up through your wrist and into your forearm. Take your time moving the energy as moving too quickly will fragment your focus and the ball will dissipate and may not merge with your own power.

Continue to ease the ball along your upper arm, through your shoulder and into your torso, where you feel the sensation of the energy merging with your fount of personal power. Feel your entire being accepting the energy from the object and merge it with your own.

This is a process that you can use when seeking to draw power for spell casting or magickal workings from an outside source such as the natural environment.

Remember to record the time and date of the magickal working in your journal, along with a description or sketch of the item from which you drew the power, and what element corresponded with that item. Include any note pertaining to yourself, your personal energy level, and the environmental conditions at the time of the working, as they may have influenced your outcome.

Chapter 12

The Witch's Year

Human beings have gone to great lengths to establish rituals, rites, ceremonies, festivals, and feasts to honor the continuous cycle of life and to worship the gods that they perceived controlled the cycle. The beliefs and teachings of a tradition or culture can be seen in these gatherings as they are manifested within the behaviors practiced and words spoken during the rites. These ceremonies are intended to strengthen the participants' understanding and faith in their own beliefs as well as nurture the relationships they have with the gods and Ancestors.

As you get *"back to the basics"* and evaluate your own practice, it's valuable for you to consider the structure of your yearly calendar, including any monthly rituals, spiritual rites, yearly ceremonies, and annual festivals or feasts that you observe, whether they are mundane or magickal in nature, as all of these sacred days will energetically influence your life and Craft.

In many ancient cultures gathering, hunting, and

agriculture were vital to the survival of the people in the community. If there was a particularly cold and snowy Winter season, there may not be enough food to last through until Spring; if they experienced a drought during the Summer the harvest may be small come Autumn, if a virus wiped out a herd of animals, there may not be enough meat to consume throughout the Winter. The community's survival was directly dependent on the natural environment in which they lived, so it is understandable that they would pay attention to the changing of the seasons and honor the shifts with a feast or festival.

Today our lives are still intimately tied to the natural world in which we reside, but our survival, at least on an individual basis, is not as dependent upon the changing seasons or weather conditions as were the lives of our ancestors. We live in a more civilized and modern society, which has given us access to many conveniences our ancestors never had the opportunity to experience. Though a blizzard in February may prove troublesomeness to the people who live in the city of Boston, Massachusetts, there isn't a fear that the entire population of that city won't make it through the Winter because every shop and store in the city will run out of food. A drought in July may cause the loss of crops and would impact the availability and price of that particular vegetable or fruit in the market, but there won't be the anxiety that any entire state in the country will starve because the size of that particular crop was smaller than usual. If a virus were to kill an entire herd of animals: chickens, or cows, or pigs, there's no real concern that there will be a lack of meat for the population of any city, town, or even state because our country, the United States of America, has a surplus of food that oftentimes goes to waste. There is more than enough food to feed the people.

We possess the modern technology of refrigeration, with which we are able to store food for future consumption, and electricity to run those refrigerators. We have the ability to climb into a car and go purchase an assortment of foods "to go", or to sit in front of a computer keyboard, gaze at the screen on our cellphone or tablet, and with almost no effort, obtain any variety of prepared food in just minutes. Our survival no longer depends on the graciousness of the seasonal weather, at least not to the degree as it once did for our ancestors.

Understanding that we are indeed Witches living in a modern society, attempting to reconstruct the rituals, rites, ceremonies, festivals, and feasts of the ancient peoples could feel inauthentic, since the motivations for those gatherings no longer apply to the Witch living and practicing today; especially where the mythology that is commonly incorporated during these individual celebrations may not align with the Witch's personal experience at that particular time or in that particular geographical location.

Ignoring the fact that you are a contemporary Witch does a great disservice to your Witchcraft. Denying that which you are, or pretending you are something you are not, is not in alignment with the first power of The Witches' Pyramid: To Know. You are not your Grandmother, nor your Great-Uncle Elphias, nor are you your Great-great-great-Aunt Sabrina. You are you, with your own experiences and perceptions gained by living in a modern era, and while it remains beneficial to maintain an energetic connection with your family history, your Beloved Dead, and with The Ancestors, it is important to remember that you can never fully understand and appreciate how they worked their magick. You are only able to read historical, and perhaps even personal accounts, but reading the words will never truly provide you with the complete picture of how they celebrated or how they practiced or even how they felt about their Craft. Your concerns may not be theirs, and many of theirs certainly won't be yours, so instead of attempting to adopt the rituals, rites, ceremonies, festivals, and feasts of the past, it would benefit you and all other modern Witches to establish her or his own Witch's Year with those holidays that resonate with their beliefs and their personal Witchcraft practices.

The Lunar Year

The thirteen full Moons are recognized, celebrated, and used within Witchcraft and other magickal practices, as the Moon is both changing, as it passes through each phase of its cycle, and yet consistent, for it is always present even when appearing invisible from the surface of the planet. The fact that the Moon does not radiate its own light, but instead reflects the Sun's light upon the Earth, is something that is often incorporated into the Witch's beliefs regarding the polarities found within the natural world, and just as the Moon influences the ocean tides, the energy of the gravitational pull also affects our human bodies, making the full Moon's appearance or disappearance in the night sky significant for the Witch or magickal practitioner.

Some Witchcraft traditions label each month's full Moon, borrowing the names from other spiritual and cultural practices, while other Witches name them according to their own beliefs, or base the names on characteristics of the geographical location in which they reside. A common reoccurring name that appears in numerous traditions and cultures is the Blue Moon.

"Blue Moon" is the name given to the second full Moon occurring in any given month of the year. This happens because the principal calendar consists of twelve months, however the lunar cycle includes thirteen full Moons. The name sometimes refers to the third of the four full Moons that occur between a Solstice and Equinox, but the name isn't given because the Moon actually appears blue in color in either situation.

Some Witches focus solely on the new or dark Moon and believe that this is a time of great importance and that honor should be given to their gods and their Witchcraft. Regardless of the tradition, practice, or magickal path, paying attention to the lunar year and the Moon's cycle can be of a great benefit to any Witch.

The Seasonal Tides

Just as the Moon has phases that we can observe and celebrate, the planet has phases as well, which are commonly known as the seasons of Winter, Spring, Summer, and Autumn. Whether your location has recognizable climate changes, such as snow during the Winter and heat during the Summer, or not, it's widely known and understood that there still exists an energetic shifting that occurs during these times. The fluctuating flow of energy maintains the balance between the polarities that exist in our natural environment and are manifested by conditions such as day and night, and birth and death. These expressions of projective and receptive energies ebb and flow like the ocean tides throughout the calendar year.

Energy of the Earth flows from East to West as it orbits around the Sun, and as the planet rotates on its axis an additional magnetic current is created. This current flows from North to South for half of the calendar year, then shifts and flows in the opposite direction, from South to North, for the other half of the year. This ongoing energetic shift is known as the Seasonal Tides and is marked by the regularly occurring Solstices and Equinoxes.

The Winter Tide begins on Winter Solstice and flows until Spring Equinox, which marks the beginning of the Spring Tide, which flows until the Summer Solstice. The Summer Tide begins on Summer Solstice, and flows until Autumn Equinox, which marks the beginning of the Autumn Tide, which flows until the Winter Solstice.

The Solstices are determined by the position of the Sun in relation to the planet. The Winter Solstice occurs when the Sun reaches its highest position in the sky from the most Northern point on the planet, while the Summer Solstice is determined to be when the Sun is at its highest position at the most Southern point on the planet. The dates of these instances vary each calendar year and will most often occur around December 21st for the Winter Solstice and June 21st for the Summer Solstice, but due to the inclusion of Leap Year, the dates may fall within the three-day range of the 20th through the 23rd.

The Equinoxes are considered to be when the Sun is perpendicular to the Earth's equator, thus equally illuminating both hemispheres of the planet. This occurs twice during a calendar year, around

March 20th for the Spring or Vernal Equinox and around September 23rd for the Autumn Equinox. The same as with the Solstices, the dates may fall within a two to three-day range due to incorporation of Leap Year.

The Wheel of the Year

The commonly known Wheel of the Year, an annual cycle of religious festivals, follows the changing of the Seasonal Tides. The Wheel, as it is presented in modern times, was first suggested by scholar Jacob Grimm in his book, *Teutonic Mythology*, but was secured in its current form in the 1950s and early 1960s by Wicca.

The holidays or sabbats that are included on The Wheel are familiar to many of us within the Pagan community, even if we don't observe or celebrate them as a part of our own practice; Samhain (October 31st), Yule (December 21st), Imbolc (February 2nd), Ostara (March 21st), Beltane (May 1st), Litha (June 21st), Lughnasadh or Lammas (August 1st), and Mabon (September 23rd).

The Wheel is divided into two equal halves: the Dark Half of the Year and the Light Half of the Year. The Dark Half of the Year, encompassing the time between Mabon and Ostara, is a time when death is witnessed in its many beautiful manifestations; from the shedding of leaves from tree branches above our heads, to the hibernation and migration of numerous species of bird and animal life. This time is a time of stillness, of rest, which is required so that the vital energy that sustains life is able to be recycled and stored, to be born again once Spring arrives.

During the Light Half of the Year, the time between Ostara and Mabon, we experience birth in its varied manifestations; from the sprouting of seeds from the depths of the Earth beneath our feet, to the renewal of life, and the return of birds and numerous other species of animals from their Winter slumber. It's a time of activity, of effort and work, which is required to bring forth our desires, both on the spiritual and mundane levels, into manifestation.

Whether you follow the traditional Wheel of the Year, or whether you observe only the Winter and Summer Solstices and Spring and Autumn Equinoxes, or just celebrate the cross quarters of Candlemas, Midsummer, Lammas, and All Hallow's Eve, it is important that these holidays hold a personal meaning for you, the Witch, who is acknowledging the day, otherwise you're just celebrating because it's expected of you and not because you're invested in the meaning of the day.

Making a personal connection with the annual festivals is dependent on the relationship you have with your Craft and your environment. If you decide to include Yule / Winter Solstice in your own Witch's Year, but where you live it's a warm seventy degrees Fahrenheit with lots of sunshine during the entire month of December, there would be an energetic dissonance for you to practice any type of snow magick or to include imagery in your ritual that focuses on the falling snow or the cold of Winter. This would not suggest that you couldn't include the Winter Solstice in your own Witch's Year, but I encourage you to find energetic connections that resonate with you and the land on which you live.

My own Witch's Year is different now than when I lived on the East Coast. In Massachusetts, the temperatures during Yule were cold, sometimes below zero degrees Fahrenheit, and the landscape was often dusted with snow. Now I live in Seattle and here the temperature rarely falls below forty degrees Fahrenheit in December, and it often rains during Winter Solstice. While I felt a resonance with the traditional Wheel of the Year and all its snowy imagery and energetic connections in Massachusetts, they no longer hold truth for me, so now I focus on the themes that do: introspection, contemplation, a time of hibernation. This shift in focus has allowed me to connect to the holidays that are in alignment with my own Witchcraft practice.

Rites of Passage and Ceremonies

Your birthday or the birthday of a family member, your wedding day, the death of a Beloved, the day you dedicated yourself to your Craft; these are some common examples of personal reoccurring moments that may bring a shifting of energy that you might choose to recognize and honor with each passing year. Combining these private moments with more generally recognized energetic shifts, such as the Solstices and Equinoxes, may construct a yearly calendar that works within your Witchcraft. You may also choose to add other Rites of Passage or ceremonies that may only occur once during your lifetime, such as a job promotion, a child's high school graduation, or the birth of a grandchild, as these moments may bring energetic shifting that could be honored, if you are inclined to do so. Your calendar should reflect the tides of your life experiences. The energy of these seemingly mundane moments will not only influence the individual they are happening for, if that individual is not you directly, they will also influence you because you are energetically connected to the person, who is directly affected by the vast interconnectedness that exists within our Physical Realm of existence.

Rites of passage are present in our modern society within secular and religious communities, both nationally as well as globally. Human beings have been acknowledging the major points in a typical human life cycle: birth, adulthood, marriage, elderhood, and death, for many years. Each of these phases of lifetime hold a distinctive energetic vibration that can be harnessed by the Witch within her or his Craft, and honoring the transition from one phase to another is a practice I embrace and encourage others to as well.

Marking your personal growth in a physical way, such as a throwing a party, is a fundamental part of living within a social group; whether you consider that social group to be a small local community, like a family or a coven, or you view it from a wider perspective, such as all of humanity or The Ancestors, is irrelevant. What is significant is the act of acknowledging your growth by both you and the social group; this action is what holds the potential to energetically support you and enhance your personal power. Once you begin marking your progression within that group, you acknowledge and accept your connection, your bond to the community, and this can be of a great benefit, and yes, at times, it may prove to be a hinderance. This concept is the reason and the motive for initiation rituals, and why for some covens it is a requirement for becoming a member of their coven, but should it be of any importance for a solitary Witch? Yes, in my opinion, it should be.

Initiation

There is an idea within the Witchcraft community that an individual is only able to become Witch through the rite of Initiation, which must be performed by a Witch, who was initiated by another Witch themselves, and that there are no other ways or means beyond initiation for someone to become Witch. This idea that only a Witch can make a Witch is flawed and demands an answer to the question: "If this is a Truth, then who initiated the first Witch?"

I understand, as I am sure you do as well, that the transference of power from one Witch to another can be an amazing and powerful experience if done successfully, but the act of transferring energy to the receiving Witch does not also include the conveyance of book knowledge or wisdom. Knowledge is the direct benefit of study, and wisdom the benefit of knowledge and experience; those things must be done through work and with the applied effort of the Witch, which is achieved through practicing our Craft. It's not done through a transference performed during an initiation rite done by another Witch.

While the concept of initiation is a ceremony by which an individual is made a member of a social group, it's also a symbolic death and rebirth, which is consciously welcomed and undergone by the individual seeking admittance into that society. The idea is that once the individual is initiated, she or he will never be the same, they are transformed into a new version of themselves and have become a part of a family that they have chosen, not one dictated by genetics or a court of law. Within Witchcraft, the rite of Initiation provides the Witch with a similar sense of belonging, which can be of a great benefit, especially for a Witch without coven associations.

Initiation is the first formal meeting of Witch and the spirits of the Unseen Realms, including The Ancestors; the moment when the Witch introduces her or himself and presents their intentions for working Witchcraft. It's the time when the Witch makes their vows and dedicates their life to The Craft. The spiritual entities that the Witch evoked become aware of her or his presence and recognize their personal energies. Every act of magick that the Witch performs from that moment forward is observed, noted, and aided or hindered, by those evoked spirits; once the Witch's vows are taken a direct connection between Witch and the Unseen Realms is established.

This does not mean that a Witch who chooses not to perform a rite of Initiation will not be recognized by the spirits of the Unseen Realms, nor does it mean that the uninitiated Witch's magick is less successful, but performing a rite of Self-Initiation does create a path of least resistance for the spiritual energy to travel, thus establishing a quicker route towards the manifestation of any of the Witch's intentions.

If we consider the Witch's relationships with the entities of the Unseen Realms similar to her or his relationships with other human beings, the rite of Initiation is akin to a party that you decide to host. The spiritual entities you evoked during the rite are the party guests you invited to the party and they're the energies you wish to bond with or establish a relationship with, just as the party guests are people you'd like to have as your friends. After the initiation, it will be easier to evoke and work with those energies within your sacred space or Circle, just as after the party it would be easier to call and hang out with one of your party guests. If you had not held a rite of initiation for yourself, but summoned a spiritual entity, during a spell casting or magickal working, it would be similar to you blindly calling on the phone someone you saw walking down the street and asking them to help you move or paint your house. While that person may agree to your request, they most likely would be more willing to help you if you had already introduced yourself and began to establish some sort of friendship with them prior to the phone call.

Considering that initiation is the moment when the individual becomes a member of a group, perhaps you're asking what group is it that the solitary Witch is being initiated into, if it's not a coven? From my perspective, during the rite of Initiation, the Witch becomes a member of the extended community of Witches, including The Ancestors, those who identified as Witches that lived before you, whose spirits you align with and draw power from when you work your Craft, and it's for this reason that such a Rite of Passage is important in journey of becoming Witch.

Exercise: Create Your Calendar

In this exercise, I encourage you to create your own Witch's Calendar, writing down the days you consider important, sacred, or noteworthy, along with the reasons why you deem them as such. When considering the overall structure of your annual holidays, decide whether you will hold a preplanned ritual or celebrate in a more spontaneous manner. It would be beneficial for you to understand your reasons and purpose for each occasion as you make these decisions. Some questions to ask yourself are:

- What is the significance of this day?
- What motivates me to make a note of it?

- What is the theme of this day?
- How will I celebrate this day?
- Are there people in my life I would like to include in this celebration?
- How does this occasion energetically and / or emotionally affect me?
- How does this occasion energetically and / or emotionally affect others in my life?
- In what ways will I honor this occasion?

Your answers, if you're honest with yourself, will enable you to discover the important energy flow within your magickal life. The significant, reoccurring moments of both low and high energy, your personal ebb and flow, will enable you to work your Craft more efficiently and with greater success. Marking these moments for yourself will organically create an annual calendar that you could follow, especially if during those days you decide to recognize the occasion in some ritualized way.

Craft a personalized calendar for yourself, whether in a Word Document on the computer or in another medium, or even in a more artistic way, if you are so inclined. Regardless of the way you decide to manifest your Witch's Calendar, do so in a practical way that will enable you to realistically follow it with each passing year, but will also allow yourself the freedom to add any significant days that might appear as time passes, and to subtract any days that you feel motivated to drop because they no longer hold significance for you and your Craft.

Exercise: Rite of Self-Initiation

Before you begin the Rite of Self-Initiation, I suggest that you read through the entirety of this exercise. If you already have an established sacred space, performing this rite there is ideal. If you are a Witch who casts Circle, you should incorporate the casting where noted within the rite or where you deem appropriate.

I suggest that you begin your preparation by contemplating what your intentions are for practicing Witchcraft. Questions that I suggest you answer for yourself are:

- What is your purpose for identifying as Witch?
- How do you live as Witch?
- What is it you seek to manifest in your life?
- How will you work to manifest this?
- What is the common focus of your spells and magickal workings?

Once you have your intentions in mind, it's time to write your vows. Just as with my evocations and invocations, I find that when making a vow, writing it out is the best practice. Writing allows me to fully discover what I am willing to commit to and what I am not. It gives me the time to fully appreciate the seriousness of what I am about to promise to the Unseen Realms or to a specific god or goddess. I encourage you to write your vows in your journal, but if unprompted vows are more aligned with your Craft, then I encourage you to follow your own practice. Be aware that vocalizing your vows during the Rite of Self-Initiation is important as I have discussed in the first chapter of this book.

Consider the appropriate energetic time for your rite and mark the day. I encourage you to consult the Lunar Year, Seasonal Tides, or Wheel of the Year, if they are part of your Witch's Calendar, as well as other correspondences, such as which day of the week and Lunar cycle energetically align with the appropriate energies you wish to work with during the Rite of Self-Initiation.

When the time approaches for the rite, you will want to prepare yourself with a cleansing, in whatever way you usually cleanse yourself. I am fond of taking a ritual bath or shower with soap specifically crafted for this purpose.

Next you should enter your sacred space. If you are a Witch who casts Circle, then this is the time to do so. Once within your sacred space, you should consecrate yourself in whatever way you usually do; if you cast a Circle you should consecrate yourself before entering casting. If you don't usually consecrate yourself, take some time to consider if it might be something you'd do for this specific Rite of Initiation due to the purpose of initiation.

Perform your evocations for The Ancestors and

all other spirits that you desire to be present for your Initiation. If you work with a Matron and / or Patron, be sure to include them.

Recite aloud your vows and offer a token as a physical representation of your promise. This token should be a physical item such as: a piece of jewelry that you will wear, an object you crafted yourself that embodies your vows, a statue that you purchased for this specific rite, or other representation. This token will either be worn frequently, hold a prominent place on your altar, or placed in another position of honor in your home.

Raise energy and release the energy either towards the token, imbuing it with the energy of your vow, or draw send it to The Unseen Realms.

Take a moment to reflect on yourself and your Witchcraft.

Then petition The Ancestors and any other spirits you evoked for a blessing on you and your Craft.

After requesting the blessing, show your gratitude by giving offerings to The Ancestors and any other spirits you evoked.

Finally, release The Ancestors, the spirits, and any other energies that you evoked during the rite. If you cast a Circle, this is the time to open it.

Be sure to ground yourself and earth any excess energy that might be lingering.

Remember to record the time and date of the Rite of Self-Initiation in your journal, along with the names of the gods and spirits you evoked. Include your feelings, personal energy level, any insights you may have gained through the experience, and the environmental conditions at the time.

Chapter 13

What Lies Beyond

Our thoughts and beliefs concerning the cycle of birth, life, and death, may not be something that impacts your Witchcraft, especially if you identify as atheistic. For many Witches, considering what lies beyond the current physical incarnation does influence their practice and deserves some consideration, especially when we are attempting to reestablish your foundation as you get *"back to the basics"* of your Witchcraft.

Most of humanity is uncomfortable with change because it's the nature of change that forces us to embrace that which is unknown, but comfort can be found in viewing time as a state of being instead of a measured period during which an action or process exists. If we were able to view time as a state of being, then all that we perceived as changed in our lives would simply be a misconception, a misunderstanding of what we were witnessing, and not a permanent condition that could not be altered. When viewed in this way, there is nothing to fear, not even the idea of death, which is understood to be a permanent condition that once embraced by the physical body cannot be altered. Instead of fearing this condition, we would view it as simply a state of being, like being happy. No human is happy forever because it's an experience that our being, our spirit, is having, which can be altered and influenced by internal and external sources. This is the same with death.

Our human experience is measured by time, which we refer to as a lifetime, but time is a creation of the ever-changing present, and it is the present that divides the future potentiality from the past. In contrast to time, eternity is all time and is not subjected to the restrictions of earthly existence. The only difference between time and eternity is the existence of our perceived limitations. Once these physical restrictions and preconceived limitations are eliminated, we are able to exist within the state of all time where anything is possible. This is precisely where the Witch resides when she or he practices Witchcraft.

It is this understanding of the concepts of change and time that leads many Witches to accept the belief of reincarnation, the belief that the non-physical part of a sentient being, the spirit, at the death of the current body, returns to the Physical Realm in a new human body to live a physical incarnation again, the purpose for which is to either accumulate human experiences or to learn life lessons.

Of the Witches that hold the belief in reincarnation, there are those that also embrace the idea of transmigration, which incorporates the belief that, after physical death, the spirit is then transferred into another vessel and thus is born once more. While this belief sounds identical to reincarnation, there is a subtle difference: reincarnation specifies the rebirth of a human spirit into another human body, while transmigration does not; the once human spirit may reincarnate into the physical body of anything, a human body or the body of an animal, or an insect, or a tree, or a rock.

Whether the Witch subscribes to the concept of reincarnation or transmigration, there is an understanding that all human beings are bound by an energy with which we never separate. The belief in the eternal spirit of each human, that existed before it manifested into physical human form, and that will continue to exist even after the death of the physical body, is a theory that is easy to comprehend, because all living beings are extensions of the vast web of interconnected energy that we, as Witch, manipulate through the act of magick. We know this to be true as we experience it within our Craft and we have science to validate our beliefs. The Law of Conservation of Energy states that energy cannot be created or destroyed, it can only be redistributed or changed from one form to another, which deems reincarnation and transmigration plausible.

These cohesive extensions of the vast web of interconnected energies, or spirits, or spiritual entities, exist within another level of reality, which is understood to be the Unseen Realms of existence. The division of these realms is completely artificial and arbitrary because they're not specific locations in space, but are instead ascending vibrations of energy, the lowest vibrational degree being physical matter and the highest point being that of ether.

Within each realm there are planes, which have no real boundaries, and instead merge one into another. The totality of the planes and realms are superimposed upon each other so that they exist in the same place, at the same time, within one reality; this is where the Witch casts her or his spells and magickal workings. The realms work in cooperation as the Witch sends forth an intention, which is fueled by the Witch's power, made of their Will and emotions, which triggers the realms with a vibration that will reverberate until the desired manifestation within the Physical Realm is achieved, or the Witch's own power loses the required momentum and disintegrates.

For example, ObsidianFire has the intention to do a healing spell for her son, who has been ill for a few days. This idea, to do the healing spell, originated within the Mental Realm. When she casts her spell, her visualization of the idea, which we will now label intention, occurs within the Astral Realm. As she evokes both her Matron goddess, Aradia, and The Ancestors, spiritual energies that align with the Divine Realm and Spiritual Realm, respectively, are triggered during her evocation. The spiritual energies or entities then align her intention, the healing of her son, as it passes through the Elemental Realm, ensuring that it takes a physical form and is ultimately manifested in the Physical Realm and within the shared reality. If ObsidianFire's intention, to heal her son, doesn't manifest within the Physical Realm, then there is a strong possibility that one of the realms was not stimulated and the energy of her intention became stalled or stagnated. The reasons for such an occurrence can be reviewed in the previous chapter titled *Spell Crafting and Casting*.

The following chart is my understanding and interpretation of the realms as I have experienced them. All Realms of Existence are considered Unseen Realms with the exception of the Physical Realm.

The Realms of Existence

Divine Realm	Divinity, Universal Source, heaven, primordial forces, gods, Ancient Ones, *"the breath of life"*
Spiritual Realm	Spirits, angels, spirit guides, familiars, The Ancestors (The Mighty Dead), Ascended Masters
Mental Realm	Memory, past-lives, shared memory, ideas, thoughtforms, egregores, servitors
Astral Realm	Space, time, magick, visions, dreams, visualization, animal spirits, ghosts, Beloved Dead
Elemental Realm	Force, energy, elements (Earth, Water, Fire, Air), elementals, Nature Spirits, demons
Physical Realm	Density, matter, human senses (sight, sound, touch, taste, smell), shared physical reality

The Witch has the ability to purposely travel to the Unseen Realms of existence by shifting her or his perception and energetic vibration to be in alignment with the specific realm they wish to visit. Traveling in this way can be done through astral projection, remote viewing, shamanic journeying, which may also be referred to as astral traveling, past-life regression, channeling, and invocation. A Witch may practice all of these or none of these and some may refer to the entire process as *"riding the hedge"*, but for myself I understand that each of these practices holds a specific purpose that I find beneficial in my own Witchcraft.

Other than purposefully and consciously traveling to the Unseen Realms while maintaining an unbroken connection to the Physical Realm, each living being currently manifested in physicality will visit the Unseen Realms at the time of their death. Each and every living being was born, and the end result of all physical life is physical death. The only way in which a spiritual being is able to leave the Physical Realm once it has been manifested is through the death process. Just as birth is an act of magick, so is death.

When the Witch sends forth an intention from the Unseen Realms, fueled by their power, triggering a vibration through all the realms, the desire is that the intention will be manifested or birthed into physicality. This act of magick is reversed when the physical body dies. At death, a vibration originating from physicality is activated and reverberates through the Unseen Realms, which begins the process of reintegrating the energy of that once living being into its pure spiritual essence, allowing it to resonate once again with the Unseen Realms from which it had been born. This energy includes the intellectual and emotional memories of that individual human being or soul, which is comprised of the physical body and ethereal spirit. From our limited perception, this process doesn't happen at the moment of physical death, but transpires over a period of time. Similar to the birthing process, which typically for a human being takes around forty weeks from conception, the death process will occur over a span of time, the length of which depends on the overall state of being of the individual at the moment of their physical death.

Death is merely a change in the state of being of a specific energetic vibration or spirit. Some Witches may have the memories of previous, or congruent, physical incarnations, which are commonly described as past-life memories or the memories of their previous lifetimes. Recalling these experiences through past-life regressions can provide the Witch with a deeper understanding of the nature of their True Will. For others the experiences have the potential to create obstacles for the Witch to overcome if she or he becomes overwhelmed by the recollections or stagnated by the desire to dissect the previous life experience in search of lessons or meaning with no guarantee of finding any.

I know many Witches will consciously shift their perception from the Physical Realm to the Astral Realm during All Hallow's Eve with the expressed purpose of communicating with their Beloved Dead. It is a common belief that at this time *the veil between the worlds is the thinnest*", meaning that the energy of these two Realms are in close alignment and there is virtually no difference in the energetic vibrations between them. Therefore, communicating with the spiritual entities that exist within the Astral Realm is easily achieved. If you are a Witch who has not yet attempted spirit communication and are curious to do so, I would encourage you to take advantage of the opportunity that presents itself during this time.

All our understandings about the Unseen Realms is based entirely on shared unverifiable personal gnosis as no human being has traveled and returned with confirmable facts of what lies beyond.

Exercise: Past-Life Regression

There are a few ways in which you can experience a past life regression; one of the more common ways is through a guided meditation. If you have found a guided meditation that you like, then I encourage you to listen to it for this exercise, otherwise you can read aloud the following visualization and record yourself for playback, or simply read the visualization and perform it while in trance.

You may not gather all information about your past-life in one session. Oftentimes images from the past-life will continue to surface in your conscious mind after the trance has ended, so it is ideal to jot down these images in your journal when they come to you for further investigation.

Before you begin, consider whether you are prepared to recall and review the memories of your previous incarnation; it may not be anything you imagine for yourself, or it may include some unpleasant experiences. It's not a practice that should be taken frivolously.

I encourage you to do a personal cleansing and have some form of protection in place. If you already have an established sacred space, then performing this exercise there is ideal; or if you are a Witch who casts Circle, I encourage you to perform this regression within your Circle. You should have your journal nearby so that you can record the details of the recall. If you have a device that enables you to record yourself as you experience the regression, that is helpful as well, and I encourage you to use the device. You can transcribe notes into your journal at a later time.

It's valuable to set an alarm for yourself for the first session; thirty minutes is ideal for the bulk of the regression, but the length of time should be adjusted according to the time you require to shift into your trance state.

When the session is complete, and you've transcribed the details into your journal, it's important for you to do research and fact check. Do not skip this process and assume everything you experienced during the past-life regression was presented as truth and fact. While you are researching, keep an open mind, but remain skeptical and use discernment when attempting to piece together the clues to your past life.

Begin your regression by setting your intention. Vocalize aloud what you want to accomplish with the past-life regression. For example:

- "I want to recall the memory of my most recent past life."
- "I want to recall the memory of the past life that has the most impact on my current incarnation."

After setting your intention, enter your trance state in whatever way you have successfully done with the previous exercises, giving yourself as much time as necessary for you to completely immerse yourself.

Use the following visualization, but do not force the experience; allow it to form organically. If you find that you are having difficulty with it, then just relax and attempt the regression at another time.

At the conclusion of the past-life regression, write down everything you're able to recall from your experience, as the information will aid you with research and fact verification. Remember to record the time and date, and any notes pertaining to yourself, your personal energy level, and the environmental conditions at the time as they may have influenced the experience.

Visualization: You are slowly walking down a long corridor. You feel a cool breeze on your skin, which carries with it the scent of fresh Rosemary. There is a dim light illuminating your way, and as you walk, your footsteps echo off the walls. The corridor is so long you cannot see where it leads, but you are not afraid.

You realize that you're not alone. Someone is walking with you, to protect you on your journey. You look to your left to see your companion. Who is it?

The corridor is so long that it takes you and your companion a few minutes to come to the end. A large door stands before you with light seeping around the edges. You know that just behind this door is the gateway to your past lives. You examine the door. What color is it? What type of door is it? You reach out to touch the surface. What is the door made of?

You look for a way to open the door. Is there a handle? A knob? A latch? A button? When you locate the way in which to open the door, and if you are comfortable to do so, open it. If you are not comfortable with opening the door, tell your companion and they will return you to your conscious awareness.

You step over the threshold and into the room. Your companion joins you and waits by the door.

Locate the chair that is positioned in the center of the room in front of a very large monitor. You walk over to the chair. Laying on the seat is a remote control. You pick up the controller and sit in the chair. You feel the chair beneath you. It is comfortable.

You look at the large monitor in front of you. The screen is black. The monitor is the largest you've ever seen. It's so big that you know that if you wanted to you could step through it without a problem.

You repeat the intention that you set prior to the visualization. You glance behind you at your companion and nod. You know that your companion will protect you and that you are not afraid.

You look at the remote in your hand. You see the

numerous buttons it has: on and off, pause, stop, fast forward, and rewind. You notice it has buttons that will allow you to turn the volume up or down, and another set that allows you to zoom in and out, giving you different perspectives. You notice the weight of the controller in your hand, the smoothness of the material. It feels comfortable to hold and manipulate. You know this remote will allow you ultimate control of your past-life experience.

When you are ready to begin, point the remote at the monitor and turn it on.

A scene from one of your past lives appears on the monitor. There is no sound – just images. What do you see?

When you are comfortable and have taken in as much detail as you are able, turn up the volume. What do you hear?

When you are comfortable, and while still holding the remote, stand from the chair and walk up to the monitor. You notice that the screen is made of a thin and permeable material that will allow you to walk through it. The monitor is a portal.

You smile and reach out your empty hand. The material is cool to the touch and gently tickles the skin of your palm. When you are comfortable, walk through the veil and into your past life.

Remember that you have control of the entire experience. The remote in your hand will allow you to completely control what you see, hear, and feel. You are able to pause or stop the experience whenever you desire.

As you stand in your past life, notice the details that are available to you. Use all your five senses to experience this moment. Where are you? What does the architecture look like? What is the mode of transportation? What are you doing? What is happening around you? Who is with you?

You look for someone to speak with. You talk to them. What does your voice sound like? What language are you speaking?

Now you search for and find a mirror or reflective surface. What do you look like? What are you wearing?

You are free to explore the environment in any way you are able. Take your time. Don't rush the experience.

When you hear your alarm, push the pause or stop button on your remote and turn to your left.

You see the portal that will bring you back to your current life experience.

When you are ready, approach the portal. It bears a thin permeable veil that you are able to pass through. You take a deep breath and walk through.

You now stand in the room where you began the regression. You see that the chair sits empty and your companion is still standing at the door.

You approach the chair and sit down. You can feel the solid chair beneath you. It is comfortable.

You look at the large monitor in front of you and notice that on the screen is the last image from your past life. You take note of the details.

When you are ready, you close your eyes and breathe deeply. The deep breath returns you to a mental state of awareness.

Epilogue

Though our book journey together has come to an end, your journey as Witch has not. Each of us is constantly learning and transforming throughout our lifetime, and it is through our experiences and direct interactions with magick and the Unseen Realms that stimulates our growth as Witches. This process doesn't end with the completion of this book, or any other book, but will continue until our physical death.

It is my hope that, with the words I've written upon these pages, I've not only helped you get *"back to the basics"* of your own Witchcraft, but that I've been able to support you as you rediscovered your power and skills with magick; that you have constructed a solid foundation that you're firmly anchored within. I hope that you're actively building upon that foundation, that your practice is once again thriving, and that you recognize your personal power as you confidently continue on your journey in becoming Witch.

10,000 Witches

They will stand,
The Witches with hearts of fire
Forged blades and Wills

Awaiting instructions
From me to reveal the target,
These powerful Witches! –
And my familiar, a companion
Focused, focused upon.
He calls in his trance

Alarm warning of attack.
And I, nearly gone,
Their potent energy rising

Power in the night –
And the sound,
The ancient incantation.

In the Circle I met Queen and Hag,
Red blood, dark soil.
Io evohe

Witches like Jesus Christ, banish
The demons
Mirror is secure, unbroken

By the cacodemon's exorcism,
The power
The power of ten thousand Witches.

Author's Notes

Thank you so much for reading *Becoming Witch*. When I mentioned to friends and followers on social media that I was publishing this book, I received comments thanking me for writing it. Many of them couldn't believe that I hadn't already published a book on the topic of Witchcraft. Apparently, it was something they thought I should have done years ago. I had considered it, but honestly, I was intimidated. While I enjoy writing fiction and sharing the paranormal Witchy stories I've written about Angie Williams, writing something based in reality and in my personal beliefs about Witchcraft and magick was daunting. I'm excited that the book is finally completed, but I'm slightly anxious that it's being published.

I'm grateful that you read this book and I would love to hear what you think about the content I provided and whether the exercises were helpful. Tell me what you liked, what you found useful, even what you hated. I want to hear from you. If you're so inclined, I'd love you to leave an honest review of *Becoming Witch* on Amazon and Goodreads. If you loved it, hated it, or just found it mediocre; I would like your feedback. And please know that I will read every single review the book receives. Reviews can be difficult to get these days, so I treasure each one. If you have the time, I would appreciate the review.

If this is the first book of mine that you've read, please consider reading my other works. *A Witch's Voice* is a collection of seventy-five poems with occult themes. *Secrets of Syn: Volume I* and *II* are collections of exciting chapters in the series about

Angie Williams, who is a descendant of a family from Salem, Massachusetts. My first published novel, *The Prodigal Son*, is the story about a man's struggle with his shadows. All the titles can be found on Amazon and the links are readily available for you on the homepage of my website – www.lunarwisdom.net.

You can find me on social media in numerous places. I'm on YouTube, Instagram, TikTok, Twitter, and Facebook, where I have a group dedicated to those who are looking for support in their journey to *Becoming Witch*. I'd love it if you join me there.

Thank you for purchasing my book and for spending some of your valuable time with me. If you enjoyed the content I've provided here, please consider recommending it to another Witch, who might find it helpful.

Thank you for your support!
CricketSong

Bibliography

Auryn, Mat. "Origin of Magickal Correspondences", *Patheos*, June 3, 2018, www.patheos.com/blogs/matauryn/2018/06/03/magickal-correspondences.

Bonewits, Philip Emmons Isaac. *Real Magic: An Introductory Treatise on The Basic Principles of Yellow Magic*. Boston, MA: Samuel Weiser, Inc. 1989.

Charmed Wiki, "Personal Gain", *Fandom*, March, 18, 2020, www.charmed.fandom.com/wiki/Personal_Gain.

Crowley, Aleister. *The Book of Thoth: A Short Essay on the Tarot of the Egyptians*. York Beach, ME: Weiser Books, 2000.

———. *Magick in Theory and Practice*. New York, NY: Castle Books, 1991.

Cunningham, Scott. *Cunningham's Encyclopedia of Magical Herbs*. Woodbury, MN: Llewellyn Publications, 2010.

Drake, Gordon W.F. "The First Law of Thermodynamics", *Encyclopedia Britannica*, January, 13, 2020, ww.britannica.com/science/thermodynamics/The-first-law-of-thermodynamics#ref258541.

Farrar, Janet and Stewart. *A Witches' Bible: The Complete Witches' Handbook*. Custer, WA: Phoenix Publishing, Inc., 1996.

Hall, Nancy. "Newton's Law of Motion", *National Aeronautics and Space Administration*, May 5, 2015, www.grc.nasa.gov/www/k-12/airplane/newton.html.

Hicks, Esther and Jerry. *The Law of Attraction: The Basics of the Teachings of Abraham*. Carlsbad, CA: Hay House, Inc., 2006.

Levi, Eliphas. *Transcendental Magic: Its Doctrine and Ritual*. Translated by Arthur Edward Waite. York Beach, ME: Samuel Weiser, Inc., 1999.

Lovecraft, H. P.. *H. P. Lovecraft Tales*. Library of America. New York, NY: Literary Classics of the United States, 2005.

Lower, Steve. "The First Law of Thermodynamics", *chem1 virtual textbook: a reference text for General Chemistry*: 2018, ww.chem1.com/acad/webtext/energetics/CE-2.html#SEC1.

Mankey, Jason. *Transformative Witchcraft: The Greater Mysteries*. Woodbury, MN: Llewellyn Publications, 2019.

Mark, Joshua J. "Wheel of the Year", *Ancient History Encyclopedia*, 28 January 2019, www.ancient.eu/Wheel_of_the_Year.

Orapello, Christopher & Tara-Love Maguire. *Besom, Stang & Sword*. Newburyport, MA: Weiser Books, 2018.

Pershing, Bob M.Sc.. "The Illusion of Time: Physics Reveals Time Is Not Real", *Learning Mind*, January 26, 2016, www.learning-mind.com/illusion-of-time.

Snuffin, Michael Osiris. "On the Powers of the Sphinx: Part 1: Eliphas Levi", *Hermetic Library*, 02/27/2017, www.hermetic.com/osiris/onthepowersofthesphinx1.

———. "On the Powers of the Sphinx: Part 2: Aleister Crowley", *Hermetic Library*, 03/16/2016, www.hermetic.com/osiris/onthepowersofthesphinx2.

Warnock, Christopher, Esq. "Planetary Hours and Days", *Renaissance Astrology*, April 4, 2020, www.renaissanceastrology.com/planetaryhoursarticle.html.

Whitcomb, Bill. *The Magician's Companion: A Practical & Encyclopedic Guide to Magical & Religious Symbolism*. St. Paul, MN: Llewllyn Publications, 2004.

Index of Exercises

The Author

CricketSong, known in the mundane world as Sheri Breault Kreitner, lives with her husband, two human children, and her two fur babies, in the beautiful Pacific Northwest. She is the author of *A Witch's Voice*, a collection of pagan poetry, the ongoing fictional series *Secrets of Syn: Volume I* and *Volume II*, and the novel, *The Prodigal Son*, all of which can be purchased through Amazon.

A Pagan Witch, CricketSong has been nurturing her relationship with the Unseen Realms her entire life, which has led her down numerous spiritual paths, granting her greater insight into the nature of deity and her Witch-self. She held the position of High Priestess in Lunar Wisdom Coven from 2011 to 2016 and the hived off online Coven of the Crescent Moon from 2014 to 2016. She has been reading Tarot, Oracle, Witches' Runes, and the Crystal Ball professionally since 2006, and has been a Reader at numerous psychic fairs, and taught numerous online classes and in person workshops throughout Southeastern Massachusetts. For more information regarding Witchcraft and the magickal services CricketSong offers visit: **www.lunarwisdom.net**.

19 11 6 11 4 7 35 4 18 9 42

Secrets of Syn: Volume I & Volume II
Sheri Breault Kreitner

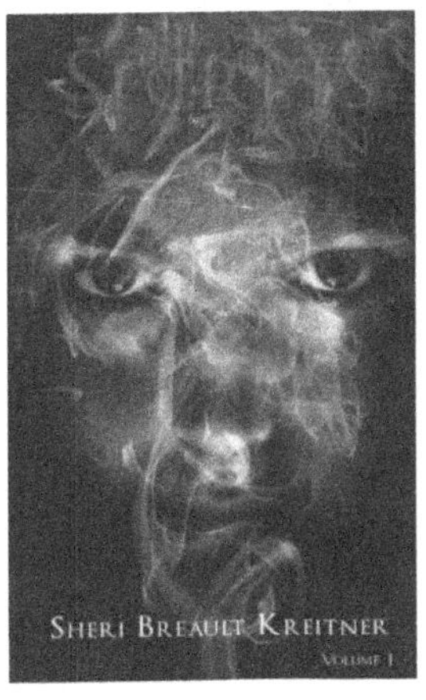 

Secrets of Syn: Volume I (chapters 1–35) and *Volume II* (chapters 36–64) of a fictional series about Angie Williams, a self-proclaimed anachronism and poetess. A descendant of the Williams of Salem Massachusetts, Angie was birthed into the modern world in a pool of blood, known as The Blood Omen. By the age of thirteen, Angie was diagnosed with paranoid schizophrenia, and by age sixteen, depression was added to her medical records, but is this unusual girl really plagued by mental illness or could there something more going on within her mind, body, and spirit? Something that has always been flowing within her bloodline?

978-1546351511, 234 pp., 5 x 8 $9.95
979-8602393767, 222 pp., 5 x 8 $9.95

Amazon and Barnes & Noble Online

A Witch's Voice
CricketSong

Within this book you will find seventy-five poems with occult themes such as: invocation, magick, necromancy, paganism, spell casting, witchcraft, and Wicca. Each poem was written with the deliberate intention of manifesting a thought that has been imbued with the emotions of the author and captured by the words she has chosen. Many of these poems written by CricketSong are accompanied by beautiful illustrations drawn by artist Nakita Melo. Whether you identify as Witch, pagan, or magickal practitioner, or are just curious about the occult, these poems are bound to entertain you.

978-1981390625, 136 pp., 8 x 10 **$19.95**

Amazon and Barnes & Noble Online

The Prodigal Son
Sheri Breault Kreitner

The Prodigal Son is a story about Luke Bennet, a renowned cardiovascular surgeon from Boston, who as a child, after experiencing the death of his father, found solace in science. Due to an unforeseen circumstance, he returns to his hometown of Tremont, and faces events that make him question the sterile life he has fashioned. While home, Luke not only reunites with old friends, he also establishes a new relationship with the exquisitely beautiful stranger named Sophia, with whom he becomes intimate. Through her unusual spiritual connection with humanity, she encourages Luke to face his faults, she helps him overcome his childhood trauma, and guides him to view life in a more balanced way.

978-1516958566, 332 pp., 5 x 8   **$14.95**

Amazon and Barnes & Noble Online

www.ingramcontent.com/pod-product-compliance
Lightning Source LLC
Chambersburg PA
CBHW072217150726
48002CB00005B/1856